W9-BFH-638

EXCERPTS FROM THE ELEMENTS OF LOGIC

FIFTH EDITION

INCLUDES STUDY GUIDE

STEPHEN F. BARKER
JOHNS HOPKINS UNIVERSITY

CHRISTOPHER DREISBACH
VILLA JULIE COLLEGE

ROBERT J. CAVALIER
CARNEGIE MELLON UNIVERSITY

McGRAW-HILL RYERSON LIMITED
Toronto Montreal New York Auckland Bogotá Caracas
Lisbon London Madrid Mexico Milan New Delhi
San Juan Singapore Sydney Tokyo

Excerpts From The Elements of Logic
Includes Study Guide
Fifth Edition

ISBN: 0-07-551030-8

1 2 3 4 5 6 7 8 9 10 5 4 3 2 1 0 9 8 7 6

Printed and bound in Canada

CONTENTS

CHAPTER 1

INTRODUCTION

1 LOGIC AND ARGUMENTS

Most courses in the curriculum of a college or university today are relatively new ones, which were not taught a few decades ago. Logic is an exception. Logic probably was taught regularly in the schools of ancient Greece, and certainly in Western Europe courses in logic have been offered to students ever since the first universities came into being some 800 or 900 years ago. What is there about logic that for so many centuries has made people regard it as deserving to be a part of higher education? The answer has two sides. Logic—the critical study of reasoning—is a subject having both theoretical interest and practical value.

On the one hand, the study of logic can be intellectually rewarding as knowledge for its own sake. This is because of the clear and systematic character of many of its principles and its close relations with basic philosophical questions and (in recent times) with the foundations of mathematics.

On the other hand, the study of logic is also of practical use. A mastery of its principles can help us to recognize and avoid mistakes in reasoning—both in the reasoning we do ourselves and in the reasoning that others use in trying to convince us of things. A person who can recognize and avoid logical mistakes in reasoning should be able to think more clearly and correctly, more soundly and surely, about any subject. To be sure, we probably should not expect the study of logic all by itself to make people who reason badly into good reasoners. Good reasoning is a very complex skill which requires sound judgment and broad knowledge concerning the subject matter about which one is going to reason. A single course in logic can hardly supply these. But it is to be expected that people who already have some skill at reasoning can improve and refine that skill through studying logic.

This book will deal with both theoretical and practical aspects of logic because both are important and both have educational value. Although it is not always easy to connect both these aspects closely together, ideally the theoretical principles of logic should be studied in living relationship with their application to actual reasoning.

Logic and Philosophy

Logic is a subject with a long history. Like so much of our intellectual heritage, it goes back to the ancient Greeks. Among the Greeks the formal study of logic began with Aristotle in the fourth century B.C. Aristotle's most important contribution to logic was his theory of the syllogism. (The nature of the syllogism will be discussed in Chapter 2.) Later, Stoic philosophers worked out some of the principles of truth-functional logic. (Truth functions will be explained in Chapter 3.)

Thinkers during the Middle Ages admired Aristotle's writings on logic far more than anyone else's, and so the medieval tradition came to regard the theory of the syllogism as the central and most important part of logic. This view persisted into the modern period. As late as the eighteenth century, the great German philosopher Kant reflected the prevailing opinion of that time when he declared that logic was a "completed science"—that is, a subject whose elements were fully understood, so that no new principles remained to be discovered in it.

Kant proved to be mistaken in this opinion, however. In the nineteenth century the Irish logician Boole showed that the field of truth functions was far richer than had previously been realized, and he devised powerful new methods for treating problems in that branch of logic as well as for generalizing the theory of the syllogism. Also, the German mathematician Frege originated the theory of quantification. (Quantification will be discussed in Chapter 4.) Then Whitehead and Russell systematized the new developments in logic in their famous work *Principia Mathematica*, written early in the twentieth century. In that work they presented the new logic in a comprehensive way, and they also tried to establish the controversial philosophical idea that the laws of pure mathematics can be derived from those of logic alone.

This modern logic does not in any way contradict the traditional aristotelian logic, when both are properly understood. However, modern logic differs from traditional aristotelian logic in two important ways. It is much more general, dealing with a far wider variety of forms of reasoning; and it uses more symbolism, its style and method being more akin to mathematics. In what follows, we shall be concerned both with the main ideas of traditional aristotelian logic and with some of the ideas of modern symbolic logic. In studying these ideas, we shall be trying always to keep in view their application to ordinary reasoning.

The more advanced logical studies nowadays have taken on a character resembling that of pure mathematics, while elementary parts of logic have their special interest because of their practical value in helping to detect mistakes in reasoning. Thus it perhaps seems that logic does not have much relation to philosophy. Yet logic has always been regarded as a branch of philosophy, and there are good reasons for this. Let us briefly consider what some of the various branches of philosophy are, and what they have in common.

Moral philosophy, or *ethics,* is the branch of philosophy that investigates the notions of good and evil, right and wrong, duty and obligation, and the like. It tries to clarify the nature of these notions in order to answer general questions about their meaning. Are there objective standards of value and rightness? How can we determine what things are good or right? What general kinds of things are good or right? In dealing with such questions, moral philosophy seeks to analyze the critical standards used in making moral judgments.

Metaphysics is the branch of philosophy that tries to understand the nature of the real universe, considered in its most general aspect. It deals with questions about what kinds of things really exist. Is everything physical, or are there real nonphysical things? What is the nature of space and time? Does everything that happens have a cause? Metaphysics seeks to handle these questions by emphasizing the standards employed in judgments about reality.

The *theory of knowledge,* or *epistemology,* is the branch of philosophy that investigates the nature and scope of knowledge. It asks what it is genuinely to know something. Can we have knowledge of things outside our own minds? Does all knowledge depend upon sense experience? The theory of knowledge seeks to analyze the standards employed in judging the genuineness of claims to the possession of knowledge.

Aesthetics is the branch of philosophy that deals with the notions of beauty and ugliness and with the value of works of art. It asks what the nature of beauty is. Are there objective standards of beauty? Can experiencing beautiful things give us insight into the nature of reality? Aesthetics tries to deal with such questions by examining the critical standards used in making judgments about what is beautiful or ugly.

Four of the main branches of philosophy have been mentioned, and they are akin to one another in important ways. They deal with questions which are extremely general. Moreover, these are not questions that can be dealt with by the methods of the special sciences: we cannot settle these questions by scientific observations or laboratory experiments. These philosophical questions are ones with which we can make headway only by reflecting upon our own standards of various kinds (our moral standards, our stan-

.dards of what counts as reality, our standards of what counts as knowledge, and so on). By obtaining a clearer view of these standards, we may be able to make progress toward unraveling philosophical questions—toward answering them in some cases, and in other cases toward clarifying the misconceptions that have given rise to the questions.

Although the study of logic differs in some ways from the pursuit of other branches of philosophy, it is no accident that in the past logic has always been classified as a branch of philosophy. Logic has a basic kinship with these other branches. Like them, it deals with some very general questions: questions about what good reasoning is and about the difference between correct and incorrect steps in thinking. Moreover, like other branches of philosophy, logic is a reflective study; experiments are not necessary, and no laboratory work is appropriate for verifying its principles. Like other branches of philosophy, logic involves the critical analysis of standards. In logic, standards of correctness in reasoning are central.

Someone might object that there is no need for a reflective, philosophical approach to reasoning, because reasoning is a phenomenon which can be studied empirically by the science of psychology. This objection rests on a misunderstanding. Of course, observations could be made and experiments conducted to find out how people reason and to discover some of the causes that make them reason as they do. But there is a difference between studying how people reason (a matter of psychology) and studying the nature of correct reasoning (a matter of logic). Logic does not undertake to describe or explain how people think; it has the different and more fundamental aim of analyzing what correct reasoning is, irrespective of whether people do, in fact, reason correctly.

Arguments

In studying logic we shall be studying the difference between good reasoning and bad. But what is reasoning? How shall we identify cases of reasoning? For the present, let us not worry about the difference between good and bad reasoning, but simply consider what reasoning is.

To start with, we can say that reasoning is a process of marshaling reasons. When one is reasoning, one is trying to put forward some things as good reasons for believing something else. Reasoning can take place when one is thinking privately to oneself, but also it can take place when one is trying to prove something to someone else. Let us look at an example of each kind.

Jane is thinking privately to herself. She remembers that last year her employer was in financial difficulty and had to cut her pay by 20 percent. Now business is better, and she is to receive a pay increase of 20 percent. This sounds good to her, but does it mean that her wages will be as large as before? She puts the facts together in her mind and realizes that the increase will be 20 percent of her present pay, and so her new wages will still be only 96 percent of her original pay. "I'll have lower pay than before the cut," she concludes.

In thinking this out, Jane is *reasoning;* she is making an *inference.* She starts from some things which she believes to be true. Then she comes to accept a consequence because she regards it as something that *follows from* these beliefs—that is, as something these beliefs provide *good reason for* accepting. Jane makes a transition from these beliefs (or *premises,* as we shall call them) to the consequence (or *conclusion,* as we shall call it). She comes to believe the conclusion because she regards the premises as showing that it is true.

The situation is a little different when the person who is to come to believe the conclusion is a different individual from the person who presents the reasoning. Suppose that Bill has always rejected astrology, while Jim has been inclined to believe in it. Bill now tries to show Jim that astrology is unreliable. Bill argues that if a person's fate were determined by the positions of the stars and planets at the time and place of the person's birth, then any two people born at the same time and place would have the same destiny. But Bill says that twins born at the same time and place sometimes grow up to have very different destinies. He says that therefore it follows that astrology is unsound.

Here, Bill wants to start from premises which Jim will accept. Then he wants to get Jim to agree that from these premises the conclusion that astrology is unreliable does follow. Bill hopes in this way to get Jim to believe this conclusion. Bill's own belief is not going to change; he presents his reasoning merely in order to change Jim's belief. If Bill is candid and sincere, he will use only premises that he himself believes; if he is not, he may use premises that he thinks will help convince Jim, even though he, Bill, does not believe them.

To generalize, we may say that *reasoning* is a process of thinking which tries to show that a conclusion should be accepted (either by the reasoner or by those being addressed) because there are good reasons indicating it to be true.

When the reasoning is put into words, we call it an argument. An argument may have just one premise, or there may be two or more. But we shall say that each step of an argument has just one conclusion. Where several conclusions are drawn, either there are several separate arguments, or there is one longer chain of argument consisting of several shorter arguments as its steps.

In the examples considered so far, the person doing the reasoning actually comes to accept the conclusion, or actually tries to get a listener to do so. The person does not just suggest a possible conclusion which someone might want to reach—if that were all that was being done, there would be a *potential* argument, but not an *actual* argument.

To illustrate this, suppose that Clara thinks to herself, "If I get a 10 percent raise for next year, and if the consumer price index rises by only 5 percent, then next year I'll be better off financially." Here Clara is trying to understand the logical connection between one possibility and another; to this extent, her thinking is like reasoning. However, she has not put forward any actual argument, for she has not asserted any premise or drawn any conclusion. She has merely made an "if-then" statement, which is not by itself an actual argument.

To be sure, her line of thought does correspond to a possible argument; that is, if she were to learn that she is getting a 10 percent raise and that consumer prices are going up by 5 percent, then she would be able to draw the conclusion that she will be better off financially. However, this mere possibility of an argument is to be distinguished from the advancing of an actual argument.[1]

What we shall mean by an *argument* (or reasoning, or inference, or proof) involves two essential features. In the first place, the person who presents the argument must be claiming that if certain things (the premises) are true, then something else (the conclusion) should be true also. That is, the person is claiming that the premises would support the conclusion, would indicate that it is true. In the second place, the person must be claiming that the premises are indeed true (perhaps the person does not *explicitly* make this claim about each of the premises, for some of them may be assumed but left unstated; but at any rate the person is *committed* to the claim that each premise is true). By making both these claims together, the person aims to give reason for accepting the conclusion as true. We shall say that there is an actual argument (or reasoning, or inference, or proof) when and only when both these claims are present.[2]

In everyday language, arguments can be expressed in many ways. Sometimes the premises are stated first; sometimes the conclusion is stated first. For example, the following are arguments:

National income for the year increased more than population did. Therefore, per capita income must have risen.

The barometer has been falling rapidly, and so there's bound to be a change of weather.

This liquid is acid, since it turns blue litmus paper red.

Octane has a higher boiling point than butane, and butane has a higher boiling point than methane; it follows that octane has a higher boiling point than methane.

There must not be any life on Venus. The atmosphere there is unsuitable, and the temperature is too extreme.

Words like "therefore," "since," and "it follows" are often signs that an argument is being presented. "Therefore" and "it follows" are used to introduce the conclusion of an argument, while "since" and "because" are used to introduce premises. Words like "must," "should," and "ought" in a sentence often serve to show that the sentence is a conclusion being derived from premises. However, none of these words is an infallible sign of an argument. In order to tell whether something that has been said embodies an argument, we need to reflect about its intended meaning. Skill and care in understanding our language are needed here; no merely mechanical rules are likely to be reliable.

Sometimes it cannot be settled whether a remark expresses an argument until we take account of the circumstances in which the remark is being made.

Suppose someone says, "The radiator of the car cracked because it froze last night and there was no antifreeze." To tell how to interpret this remark, we have to consider the circumstances under which it is made. If the listeners are not sure whether the radiator has cracked, the speaker may be making this remark in order to convince them that this has happened; in that context, the remark would express an argument with the conclusion that the radiator cracked. However, if everyone is already aware that the radiator has cracked, then a speaker who makes this remark is more likely to be trying to *explain why* the radiator cracked. If that is what is being done, the speaker's remark is a statement about the *cause* of the event, and is not an argument aiming to show that the event occurred—indeed, it is not an actual argument at all.

Often we come across remarks which are attempts to persuade us of things, yet which do not clearly state conclusions or clearly support them. Consider, for example:

Drink Extra-Light beer! It's the beer of champions.

The Dolores Speedster goes from 0 to 60 in eight seconds. You should be in the driver's seat!

Congressman Brown loves baseball, motherhood, and apple pie. He's the man for us.

Should we classify remarks like these as arguments? In the first place, to regard them as arguments in the logical sense we would need to be able to pick out their conclusions. But what conclusion is the first speaker trying to establish? That Extra-Light is the best tasting beer, the most wholesome beer, the beer with most prestige, or what? In this example no one conclusion can be pinned down, and it is the same with the other examples. In the second place, even if we were able to formulate some hazy 'conclusion' for each example, it is far from clear that the speaker is even trying to say anything to support the supposed 'conclusion.' Thus in these examples the 'conclusions' are very unclear, and the 'premises' amount to very little. If we were to classify these examples as arguments, we would have to regard them as very weak, unsatisfactory arguments. Yet surely it would be unfair to these speakers to criticize them for offering bad arguments, when they do not seem to be trying to offer good arguments. It is better to regard examples like these merely as efforts at *verbal persuasion*, and not as actual arguments.

Longer arguments often consist of chains of steps, with the conclusion of one step serving as a premise for another step. To understand such an argument, we need to recognize how its parts are connected together. As an example, let us consider the following argument.

> When a lawyer suspects a client of being guilty, is it ethical for the lawyer to conduct a vigorous defense? Yes, it is ethical. Look here: Being ethical as a lawyer involves playing by the rules of our adversary system. According to our system, every defendant has the right to a fair trial. It follows that even a defendant everyone thinks is guilty has that right. Now, you can't have a fair trial without a vigorous defense. So even if everyone thinks a defendant is guilty, under our system the defendant still has to be given a vigorous defense. This couldn't be done if no ethical lawyer would take the case and defend it vigorously. So you see it can be ethically all right for lawyers to defend vigorously clients whom they suspect of being guilty.

A number of different points are present in this argument.

1 Even when a lawyer suspects a client of being guilty, it is ethical for the lawyer to conduct a vigorous defense.

2 Ethical lawyers play by the rules of our adversary system.

3 According to our system, every defendant has the right to a fair trial.

4 A defendant everyone thinks is guilty has that right.

5 You can't have a fair trial without a vigorous defense.

6 Even if everyone thinks a defendant is guilty, under our system the defendant has to be given a vigorous defense.

7 The defendant couldn't be given a vigorous defense if no ethical lawyer would take the case and act vigorously.

For present purposes we are not trying to decide just how good an argument this is; here we merely want to unravel its structure. What is the conclusion, and what are the premises? Point 1 is the conclusion which the speaker is trying to establish. Points 2, 3, 5, and 7 are the basic premises. Points 4 and 6 are intermediate conclusions; 4 is obtained from 3, while 6 is obtained from 4 and 5 together. Using an arrow to indicate the direction of inference, we can diagram the structure of the argument in this way:

$$3 \rightarrow \left.\begin{array}{c} 4 \\ 5 \end{array}\right\} \rightarrow \left.\begin{array}{c} 6 \\ 7 \\ 2 \end{array}\right\} \rightarrow 1$$

Here the three arrows indicate three steps in the reasoning. From 3, 4 is derived. From 4 and 5 together, 6 is derived. From 6, 7, and 2 together the conclusion, 1, is derived. The diagram depicts this structure of the reasoning.

If we look for arguments in the books we read and in the conversations we hear, we shall find that most writers and speakers are presenting actual arguments only a small fraction of the time. The larger portion of most discourse consists merely of separate statements made one after another, without any of them being put forward as reasons on the basis of which others are arrived at. This is perfectly appropriate much of the time. But where the statements made are dubious or controversial, arguments are needed. Without even considering the arguments pro and con, thoughtless people make up their minds whether to accept dubious or controversial assertions. But reasonable people will want to think over the arguments before accepting or rejecting such assertions, and for the most part they will want to make it their practice to believe in accordance with the best arguments.

EXERCISE 1

*A Interpreting each example in the way it is most likely to be intended, say whether it contains an actual argument. If so, what is the conclusion and what are the premises?

1 Dogs always like bones, so her dog surely will like these bones I've brought.
2 The kiwi isn't a mammal. It's native to New Zealand, and no mammals are.
3 Your honor, the traffic light wasn't red when I went through. I swear it. Believe me, I'm telling the absolute truth.
4 The weather is going to change, because the barometer has fallen sharply.
5 The car stopped running because the gas line was clogged.
6 Anywhere corn grows, soybeans can grow. Corn grows in Iowa, so soybeans can grow there too.
7 They're a healthy, happy family. They eat Shredded Oats. Do you?
8 Everyone at the lecture is bored. No one who's bored is listening. Therefore, no one at the lecture is listening.
9 Matt mounted his horse sadly. Dusk was beginning to fall. He rode off into the twilight.
10 You'd do well to put aluminum siding on that old house of yours. It's not too expensive and never needs repainting.
11 That woman was always complaining, so I packed up and left her.
12 Since inflation is accelerating, the price of gold will increase.
13 Since he had that auto accident, he's been walking with a cane.
14 My former doctor kept telling me to go on a diet, so I changed doctors.
15 Lead is dense and comparatively inexpensive, so it is practical to use as shielding against radiation.
16 Nome is north of Anchorage, and Anchorage is north of Juneau. Hence, Nome is north of Juneau.
17 If all that oil is spilled into the river, serious pollution will occur.
18 There aren't any of my books that I won't gladly lend.
19 If you want to make an omelet, you have to break eggs.
20 No matter how severe the challenges we encounter, we shall continue to fight the good fight. We must emerge victorious in the end.

B Diagram the structure of each of the following arguments.

1 It's no use going to the bank today. This is a legal holiday. The bank will be closed. Banks always close on legal holidays.

2 There's no way we can get to Leadville on time, if we stop at Silverton. When we stop at Silverton we always end up having to stay overnight with your cousins. If we don't get to Leadville on time, we'll miss the auction. So either we stop at Silverton or we miss the auction.

3 The car is worth the price you're asking only if it's in mint condition. But its condition isn't that good. It looks as though the frame has been twisted in a collision. So the car isn't worth your price.

4 Janice is well qualified to work for you as a section head. The job requires understanding of management strategies and experience in handling people. She holds an M.B.A., so you can count on her to understand management strategies; and certainly she is experienced in dealing with people, because she served successfully for two years as personnel director in our Dallas office.

5 Theism is the viewpoint that involves belief in a supernatural God. Now, a supernatural God couldn't be a physical being. That is why you cannot be both a theist and a materialist, for materialists hold that there aren't any beings other than physical ones.

C Construct a clear step-by-step argument establishing what the answer is to each of the following problems.

1 Abe, Bill, Cindy, Don, and Ella each lives in a different city. Abe lives in the third of these cities to the west of Cindy. Bill or Don or Ella lives to the east of Cindy just in case Abe does so as well. Ella lives east of Bill and of Don. Don lives west of Bill if Cindy lives east of Ella. The cities are Albany, Boston, Chicago, Detroit, and El Paso. Who lives where?

2 Each speaker says the following and nothing more: Ali says that Bo speaks falsely; Bo says that Charlie speaks falsely; Charlie says that both Ali and Bo speak falsely. Who speaks truly?

3 There's to be a surprise fire drill one weekday next week. The following statements have been made about it: "It'll be Monday"; "It'll be Tuesday"; "It'll be Wednesday"; "It won't be Monday, Tuesday, or Wednesday"; "It won't be Thursday." One and only one of these statements is true. When will the fire drill be?

4 Theo wants to marry a girl who is blonde, beautiful, and rich. He knows only four girls: Angie, Betsy, Chris, and Deb. Of them, three are blonde, two are rich, and one is beautiful, though each has at least one of these traits. Angie and Betsy are alike in net worth; Betsy and Chris have the same hair color; Chris and Deb differ in hair color. Whom should Theo marry?

†D For each of the following examples, say whether the author presents an actual argument. If so, point out the conclusion and the premises. Identify any intermediate steps of reasoning.

1 You admit then that I believe in divinities. Now, if these divinities are a species of gods, then there is my proof that...I do believe in gods. If, on the other hand, these divinities are sons of gods, their natural sons, as it were, by nymphs or some other mortal mothers, as rumor makes them, why, then, let me ask you, is there anyone in the world who could suppose that there are sons of gods and at the same time that there are no gods?   PLATO, *Apology*

2 I had a farm in Africa, at the foot of the Ngong Hills. The Equator runs across these highlands, a hundred miles to the North, and the farm lay at an altitude of over six thousand feet.   ISAK DINESEN, *Out of Africa*

3 Spriggs,...having fallen into a fire when drunk, had had one eye burnt out, one cheek burnt through, and one arm nearly burnt off, and, therefore, in regard to personal appearance, was not the most prepossessing of men.
                                        ANTHONY TROLLOPE, *The Warden*

4 Therefore it is clear that, as the soul needs only the Word of God for its life and righteousness, so it is justified by faith alone and not any works; for if it could be justified by anything else, it would not need the Word, and consequently it would not need faith.
                            MARTIN LUTHER, *The Freedom of a Christian*

5 In peace and prosperity states and individuals have better sentiments, because they do not find themselves suddenly confronted with imperious necessities; but war takes away the easy supply of daily wants, and so proves a rough master, that brings most men's character to a level with their fortunes.   THUCYDIDES, *The Peloponnesian War*

6 I do not think that one should have children. I observe in the acquisition of children many risks and many griefs, whereas a harvest is rare, and even where it exists, it is thin and poor.
                                    DEMOCRITUS, *Fragments on Ethics*

7 To be opinionated is most shameful, for two reasons: Not only can a person not learn what he is convinced he already knows, but also the very rashness itself is a mark of a mind that is not properly disposed.
                                        AUGUSTINE, *On the Teacher*

8 *Nora:* And I—how am I fitted to bring up the children?...I am not fit for the task. There is another task I must undertake first. I must try to educate myself—you are not the man to help me in that...And that is why I am going to leave you now.   HENRIK IBSEN, *A Doll's House*

9 Every man has a right to risk his own life in order to preserve it. Has it ever been said that a man who throws himself out of the window to escape from a fire is guilty of suicide? Has such a crime ever been laid to the charge of him who perished in a storm because, when he went on board, he knew of the danger?   JEAN-JACQUES ROUSSEAU, *The Social Contract*

10 Although animals do nothing which can convince us that they think, nevertheless, because their bodily organs are not very different from ours, we might conjecture that there was some faculty of thought joined to these organs, as we experience in ourselves, although theirs be much less perfect, to which I have nothing to reply, except that, if they could think as we do, they would have an immortal soul as well as we, which is not likely, because there is no reason for believing it of some animals without believing it of all, and there are many of them too imperfect to make it possible to believe it of them, such as oysters, sponges, etc.
                        RENE DESCARTES, *Letter to Marquis of Newcastle*

2   DEDUCTION AND VALIDITY

In order to understand arguments better, we shall divide them into various types which can be considered separately. Let us begin by distinguishing between what are called deductive and what are called inductive arguments. There are good and bad arguments belonging to each type.

Deductive and Inductive Arguments

The basic distinction between deductive and inductive arguments has to do with the type of logical link that is supposed to hold between the premises and the conclusion. Sometimes a person who argues is claiming that the truth of the premises is absolutely sufficient to establish the truth of the conclusion. In other cases the claim is not that the link is this strong, but merely that the link is strong enough so that the premises do support or confirm the conclusion, making it reasonable to believe.

Here is an argument of the first sort:

Whenever it's winter in New York, it's summer in Rio. It's winter now in New York, and so it's summer now in Rio.

Here we have an argument that is *demonstrative*. That is, it has premises such that if they are true, they absolutely ensure the truth of the conclusion. Knowing that the premises are true would give us completely sufficient reason for believing the conclusion. Indeed, it would be inconsistent for anyone who accepts the premises as true to regard the conclusion as false. This is a *deductive* argument.

An argument that succeeds in being demonstrative has the strongest kind of logical connection between its premises and its conclusion, and so in that respect it is a good argument. But we also want to allow for the possibility that a deductive argument can be a bad argument, lacking a sufficiently strong logical connection between its premises and its conclusion. We shall therefore say that if the speaker puts forward the premises with the claim that the conclusion strictly follows from them, then also the argument is deductive, even when this claim is mistaken. For example, suppose someone argues:

Whenever it's raining, the streets are slippery; and the streets are slippery now, and so it's got to be raining now.

Here the wording suggests that the speaker is claiming that the premises are strictly sufficient to establish the conclusion (of course we may have to investigate the circumstances in which the remark is voiced, in order to tell for sure what the speaker's intentions are). If this is the correct interpretation of what the speaker is claiming, then we shall classify the argument as deductive. Of course it is a bad deductive argument, for the truth of the premises in this case does not absolutely guarantee the truth of the conclusion.

In general, then, we shall say that an argument is deductive when and only when either its premises if true would be absolutely sufficient to guarantee the truth of the conclusion or at any rate the speaker claims that they are sufficient in this way.

Now let us look at some contrasting examples:

Jim belongs to the National Rifle Association. Most members of the NRA oppose gun control. So probably Jim opposes gun control.

When I bought shoes of this brand and style before, they lasted a long time. If I buy another pair, most likely they will last a long time too.

We shall regard the sentences "Jim opposes gun control" and "If I buy another pair, they will last a long time" as the conclusions of the arguments. We interpret the words "probably" and "most likely" not as parts of the conclusions but as indicators of the degree of connection claimed to hold between premises and conclusions.

Under the likeliest interpretation of them, these last two arguments are not deductive. That is, their conclusions do not strictly follow from their premises, nor is the speaker claiming this. Moreover, in each case the conclusion makes some prediction or expresses some conjecture that we can find out about by further observations (we can wait until there is an election in which gun control is an issue and then observe how Jim votes; we can test the shoes over a period of time to discover how long they wear). Arguments like this we shall call *inductive* arguments. That is, inductive arguments are arguments whose conclusions do not strictly follow from the premises and are not claimed to do so, but whose conclusions can in principle be tested by further observations.[3]

The conclusion of an inductive argument does not strictly follow from the premises, and this means that there would be no contradiction involved in accepting the premises but denying the conclusion. The premises may render the conclusion probable—but always it remains logically possible that the premises are true and the conclusion nevertheless false.

Deductive and inductive arguments are the only types of argument that are much studied by logicians; indeed, they have studied deduction much more extensively than induction, because deductive reasoning can be described more readily in terms of definite general rules. Whether there is any genuine reasoning that is neither deductive nor inductive is a question to which we shall briefly return later (in Chapter 8).

In practice, when we encounter arguments, we cannot always manage to classify them definitely as deductive or as inductive. This is because sometimes the person who presents an argument does not make clear how tight a link is being claimed to exist between premises and conclusion (the speaker may even be unclear in his or her own mind about this question). In such cases we can at least consider which way of classifying the argument would fit in better with what the speaker would be justified in claiming.

Notice that the conclusion of a comparatively good deductive argument is not necessarily established with any greater certainty than it would have if it were the conclusion of a comparatively good inductive argument. How firmly the conclusion is established depends both on how tight the link is between premises and conclusion and on how certain the premises are to start with. Often, if we want a deductive proof of a conclusion, we have to be satisfied to start with premises that are less certain than other premises we could employ if we were constructing an inductive argument for that same conclusion. For example, suppose that we are trying to establish the conclusion "No marsupials are carnivorous." One way would be to employ a deductive argument; perhaps "All marsupials are herbivorous; nothing herbivorous is carnivorous; so no marsupials are carnivorous." Another way would be to employ an inductive argument, such as "I've observed several kinds of marsupials and never found any to be carnivorous, and so probably no marsupials are carnivorous." The deductive argument has a much tighter link between premises and conclusion than the inductive argument has, but it has to employ premises which are much more doubtful than those the inductive argument uses. So let us avoid the idea that deductive conclusions are always, or even usually, more certain than inductive conclusions.

Truth and Validity

Truth is a feature relating to the premises and conclusions of arguments. Validity is a feature of whole arguments themselves, having to do with how tightly the premises are connected with the conclusion. These two notions are interrelated in important ways, but they are not the same.

What sort of items can be the premises and conclusions of arguments? We shall call them sentences. A *sentence* may be defined roughly as a series of words that form a complete utterance in accordance with the conventions of language. The kinds of sentences with which we are concerned, the ones that can serve as premises and conclusions in arguments, are used to say what is *true or false*. Ordinarily they are what grammarians call declarative sentences. Other kinds of sentences, such as questions or exclamations, usually would not be appropriate as premises or conclusions of arguments, for typically they are not used to say anything true or false. In some cases, however, a question or exclamation can be used to do this ("What a rainy day!" and "Isn't this a rainy day?" each can be used to convey the information that this is a rainy day).[4]

Naturally, a sentence that is a premise in one argument may be a conclusion in some other argument. Suppose I am trying to prove a conclusion, and in doing so I advance an argument that uses another sentence as its premise. My opponent, even if he grants that my conclusion follows from my premise, may question whether my premise is true; he may say that he will not accept my conclusion until I prove my premise. If he challenges my premise in this way, I may be able to meet his challenge by constructing a new argument to establish that premise; that is, a new argument which will have as its conclusion the premise of the first argument. I would hope to be able to choose as the premise of my new argument something my opponent will not challenge; but if he challenges the premise of the new argument also, then perhaps I can prove it too.

We noted earlier that an argument has two essential features: (1) The speaker who presents the argument is claiming that the premises are true, and (2) is also claiming that if these premises are true, the conclusion should be true too (the strength of the logical link can vary, as we noticed). Every argument, whether good or bad, must have both these features if it is to be an actual argument. Now we can see that there are two chief ways in which a person can go wrong and advance an unsatisfactory argument. On the one hand, the person presenting the argument may be going wrong in claiming that the premises are true (perhaps the premises are not all true, or perhaps it is not really known whether they are true). Or the person may go wrong by claiming that there is a stronger connection between premises and conclusion than is really there. Logic is more concerned with mistakes of this second kind than it is with mistakes of the first kind. It is not the business of logic to tell us what premises we should start with in our thinking (except that our premises should be logically consistent with one another); but it is the business of logic to help us see how conclusions ought to be connected with their premises.

The first kind of mistake is the mistake of using false sentences (or sentences not known to be true) as premises. Now, sentences can be said to be true or false, but whole arguments should not be spoken of as true or false. When the premises of an argument are linked to the conclusion in the right sort of logical way, the argument is called *valid*.[5] That is, in a valid argument the premises really do support the conclusion; if the premises are true, then the conclusion should be true too. An argument is *invalid* if its premises are not related to its conclusion in this way. Thus the second kind of mistake is the mistake of employing an argument that is invalid.

To see clearly that there is a difference between truth and validity, let us think about deductive arguments. (For inductive arguments, truth and validity are related in a somewhat more complicated way, which will be discussed in Chapter 7.) A deductive argument is valid provided that if its premises are true, its conclusion must necessarily be true also. Notice, however, that even when a deductive argument is valid, its conclusion can still be false. For example, the argument "All whales are fish; no fish are mammals; therefore, no whales are mammals" is an argument that is deductively valid; that is, if the premises were all true, the conclusion would have to be true also. But the conclusion is false, and that is possible because the premises are not all true.

Also we should notice that a conclusion invalidly reached may happen to be true. For example, the argument "All whales are animals; all mammals are animals; therefore all whales are mammals" is an argument whose conclusion happens to be true even though the argument is invalid. (If someone does not see that this example is invalid, a good way to respond is to make use of an *analogy*. We say to the person, "If you think that this is valid, then you might as well say that 'All pigs have legs and all birds have legs, and so all pigs are birds' is a valid argument." In this way we are likely to be able to show the person that in this style of reasoning the premises do not support the conclusion with the strictness that valid deduction requires.)

The one thing that cannot happen with deductive arguments is for a false conclusion to be validly deduced from premises all of which are true. This cannot happen because it would violate our definition of what we mean when we call a deductive argument valid.

One further bit of terminology: in ordinary language the word "imply" means to hint or to suggest; but in logic this word is used in a different and stronger sense. When we say that the premises of an argument *imply* the conclusion, we mean that the argument is a valid deductive argument. More generally, to say that one sentence or group of sentences implies another sentence means that if the former are true, the latter must necessarily be true also.[6] (We do not say that the premises *infer* the conclusion in a valid deductive argument, because people, not premises, make inferences. Implication is a logical relation that can hold between sentences; inference is an act that people perform when they derive one sentence from another.)

EXERCISE 2

*A For each example, decide whether it contains an argument. If it does, decide whether it makes better sense to interpret the argument as deductive or as inductive; also identify the conclusion and the premises.

1 Our customers always are satisfied. You've bought our product. Therefore, you'll be satisfied too.

2 Our past customers always have been satisfied. You've bought our product. Therefore, you'll be satisfied too.

3 It doesn't snow in Jamaica, because that's in the Caribbean, and it never snows anywhere in the Caribbean.

4 Snow never has been observed in Aruba. So, if you go there this winter, you won't encounter snow.

5 For the party, we need one chair per guest. 38 were invited, and 12 of them are not coming. We have two dozen chairs. So we need 2 more chairs.

6 Only those who've registered may vote in the election. Will hasn't registered, so he isn't permitted to vote.

7 Most large flightless birds are very fast runners. So probably the Moa, which was large and flightless, was a fast runner.

8 The cakes she's baked according to her grandmother's recipe came out well. So probably today's cake will come out well, as she's making it according to that same recipe.

9 Whenever the public fears deflation, demand for gold declines. When demand declines, the price falls. So the price of gold falls whenever the public fears deflation.

10 It's probably going to rain, for the cows are lying down, and almost always when the cows are lying down it rains.

11 If it's a Taurus, it's a Ford. And it is a Taurus. So it must certainly be a Ford.

12 If it's a Taurus, it's a Ford. And it is a Ford. Therefore, it must certainly be a Taurus.

13 No Unitarians are Trinitarians; all Catholics are Trinitarians; so no Catholics are Unitarians.

14 All Sunnis are Moslems, and all Shiites are Moslems; so all Shiites are Sunnis.

15 Small tremors have been getting more frequent, and usually that's a sign of an impending earthquake. So probably there'll be a quake before long.

B Each of the following is to be regarded as a deductive argument. In each case, is the argument valid? Are its premises all true? Is its conclusion true? Notice how each example differs from every other.

1 All Italians are Europeans, and all Venetians are Italians. Therefore, all Venetians are Europeans.

2 All Italians are Europeans, and all Venetians are Europeans. Therefore, all Venetians are Italians.

3 All Italians are Asians, and all Venetians are Italians. Therefore, all Venetians are Asians.

4 All Italians are Asians, and all Venetians are Asians. Therefore, all Italians are Venetians.

5 All Italians are Asians, and all Venetians are Asians. Therefore, all Venetians are Italians.

6 All Italians are Asians, and all Japanese are Italians. Therefore, all Japanese are Asians.

7 All Italians are Europeans, and all Venetians are Europeans. Therefore, all Italians are Venetians.

†C For each example, what is the structure of the reasoning, and does it make better sense to interpret it as deductive or as inductive?

1 A jagged stone was lying among the moss..."This may interest you, Lestrade," he said..."The murder was done with it...The grass was growing under it. It had only lain there a few days. There was no sign of a place whence it had been taken. It corresponds with the injuries. There is no sign of any other weapon."

A. CONAN DOYLE, "The Boscombe Valley Mystery"

2 A dog, used to eating eggs, saw an oyster, and, opening his mouth to its widest extent, swallowed it it down with the utmost relish, supposing it to be an egg. Soon afterwards suffering great pain in his stomach, he said: "I deserve all this torment, for my folly in thinking that everything round must be an egg."

AESOP, *Fables*

3 A struggle for existence inevitably follows from the high rate at which all organic beings tend to increase...As more individuals are produced than can possibly survive, there must in every case be a struggle for existence, either one individual with another of the same species, or with individuals of distinct species, or with the physical conditions of life.

DARWIN, *The Origin of Species*

4 ...You are wise,
Or else you love not; for to be wise and love

Exceeds man's might; that dwells with gods above.
SHAKESPEARE, *Troilus and Cressida*

5 It is necessary that the land and the surrounding waters have the figure which the shadow of the earth casts, for at the time of an eclipse it projects on the moon the circumference of a perfect circle. Therefore, the earth is not a plane, as Empedocles and Anaximenes opined...or again a cylinder, as Anaximander,...but it is perfectly round.
COPERNICUS, *On the Revolutions of the Celestial Spheres*

6 The nature of the mind and soul is bodily; for when it is seen to push the limbs, rouse the body from sleep, and alter the countenance and guide and turn about the whole man, and when we see that none of these effects can take place without touch nor touch without body, must we not admit that the mind and the soul are of a bodily nature?
LUCRETIUS, *On the Nature of Things*

7 "Sperrit? Well, maybe," he said. "But there's one thing not clear to me. There was an echo. Now, no man ever seen a sperrit with a shadow; well, then, what's he doing with an echo to him, I should like to know? That ain't in nature surely?"   R. L. STEVENSON, *Treasure Island*

8 [Flaubert in his] letters to Louise Colet...boasts of amorous exploits, which must be true, since he is addressing the only person who can be both witness and judge of them.
JEAN-PAUL SARTRE, *Search for a Method*

3 EMPIRICAL AND NECESSARY SENTENCES

The sentences that serve as premises of an argument are supposed to be true, and their truth is supposed to give us reason for accepting as true the sentence which is the conclusion. However, sentences are not all alike. Let us notice two important types of sentences which differ with respect to how we can know whether they are true.

Most of the sentences we ordinarily deal with are *empirical* (this means "based on experience"). Consider a few examples:

Lead is cheaper than copper.
Some pigs can fly.
Caesar conquered Gaul.
Ted's age plus Jim's age equals thirty-two.

Each of these sample sentences is somehow based on experience; but in what sense? Not merely in the rather uninteresting sense that to know whether the sentence is true one must have had the experience involved in learning the meanings of the words—for us, all sentences are "based on experience" to this minimal extent. No, these sentences are connected with experience in a stronger sense: to know that one of these sentences is true or that it is false, we must possess *evidence drawn from experience*—sensory evidence concerning what has been seen or heard or felt or smelled or tasted. This evidence might consist of direct observations one has made for oneself, or it might be more indirect, consisting, say, of what one has heard concerning what others have seen. Now, to be sure, a person lacking such evidence drawn from experience could still *believe* it to be true that lead is cheaper than copper, or *believe* it to be false that some pigs can fly; but such a person would not *know* these things, because it would be merely accidental whether the person's beliefs were correct. For us, beliefs about such matters cannot be knowledge unless we have properly based them on direct or indirect evidence obtained by use of our senses.

Thus merely understanding the meaning of an empirical sentence is not sufficient to enable us to know whether it is true. In addition to understanding the sentence, we must have sensory experience which we can use to determine whether what the sentence says is true. Empirical sentences are said to be known *a posteriori* ("afterward"), because we can know whether they are true only after obtaining appropriate experience. Also, empirical sentences are said to be *contingent*, in that their truth or falsity depends on more than their meaning; an empirical sentence is a sentence which, if true, might conceivably have been false, or which, if false, might conceivably have been true.

However, there is another type of sentence which can be known to be true or to be false without reliance upon sensory evidence. Such sentences are said to be knowable *a priori* ("beforehand"), because we can know whether they are true before we observe the phenomena of which they speak. Among sentences of this type, we shall concentrate on *necessary* sentences: sentences that are necessarily true because to deny them would involve an inconsistency, or that are necessarily false because to affirm them would involve an inconsistency.[7] Some examples:

Snow is white, or it is not.
All dogs are animals.
Fifteen plus seventeen equals thirty two.
Caesar conquered Gaul, but Caesar didn't conquer Gaul.

When these sentences are understood straightforwardly in their likeliest senses, the first, second, and third are necessarily true. To deny them would involve inconsistency—something illogical or inconceivable such as snow that is both white and not white or dogs that are not animals. The fourth sentence is necessarily false. To affirm it would involve an inconsistency (Caesar's both doing and not doing the same thing). And all four sentences are a priori, since there is no need to have evidence from sense experience in order to know whether they are true. One can come to know whether they are true just by understanding the meanings of the words employed and by reflecting upon what the sentences say. For example, by understanding the meanings of the words involved, we realize that it would not be literally true to call something a dog unless it were an animal. This enables us to know a priori that all dogs are necessarily animals. No sense experience, beyond what was involved in learning the meanings of the words, is required in order to enable us to know this.

In logic we are interested in learning to tell the difference between arguments that are valid and arguments that are invalid. But to understand that the argument "No birds are cold-blooded; all reptiles are cold-blooded; therefore no reptiles are birds" is a valid deductive argument amounts to the same thing as to understand that the sentence "If no birds are cold-blooded and all reptiles are cold-blooded, then no reptiles are birds" is a necessarily true sentence. The argument differs from the sentence in that it consists of a series of sentences (premises that are asserted and a conclusion that is derived). But to recognize the deductive validity of the argument is to recognize that if the premises are true, then the conclusion must be true too; and this amounts to the same thing as recognizing that the "if-then" sentence is necessarily true.

Thus in logic we are very much concerned with necessary sentences. We are especially concerned with sentences that are necessarily true in virtue of their *logical forms*, that is, because of the ways in which certain logical words such as "all," "some," and "not" are arranged in them. The logical form "If no...are *** and all --- are ***, then no --- are..." is such that, with whatever words or phrases we consistently fill in the gaps (provided we make sense), we always get an overall "if-then" sentence that is true. Regardless of its subject matter, any sentence of this form has to be true. Thus we say that the "if-then" sentence we were considering in the previous paragraph is true in virtue of its logical form, and the corresponding argument is valid in virtue of its logical form. We shall learn more about logical form in later chapters.

Returning to our distinction between empirical and necessary sentences, we must recognize that this is not an absolutely precise distinction. There are plenty of borderline cases of sentences that do not clearly belong in one category rather than in the other. For example, consider the sentence "All spiders have eight legs." When straightforwardly understood, is this a necessary a priori truth, or is it an empirical truth? Is there or is there not an inconsistency involved in supposing that there might be a species of spiders that did not have eight legs? (Suppose explorers found a species of creatures that looked like spiders, behaved like spiders, and were directly descended from spiders—but which had evolved ten legs instead of eight. Would it be incorrect to call such creatures spiders?) There are no definite answers to these questions, because the word "spider" is somewhat indefinite in its meaning. Because of this indefiniteness, there is no answer to the question whether the sentence as ordinarily understood is necessary or empirical. Of course we could decide to change or sharpen the meaning we attach to the word "spider"; then the sentence could become either definitely empirical or definitely necessary—but it is not definitely either one as matters stand.

Thus some sentences cannot be definitely classified as necessary or empirical. However, the distinction between necessary and empirical sentences still has value, in spite of such borderline cases, for many sentences with which we are ordinarily concerned are not borderline cases and do fit definitely into one but not the other of these categories. And even with sentences that do not fit definitely into either category, it can often be enlightening to ask: *To what extent* are they necessary? To what extent are they empirical? How could they be understood so as to be necessary? How could they be understood so as to be empirical? By thinking about sentences in this way we often come to comprehend them better.

Moreover, the distinction between necessary and empirical sentences is of interest in two further ways, one theoretical and the other practical.

First, the distinction draws to our attention a philosophical difference between two types of knowledge: the a priori knowledge involved in logic and mathematics, on the one hand, and the empirical knowledge involved in the experimental sciences, on the other hand. Sentences which express the laws of physics, chemistry, and other experimental sciences typically are empirical sentences. They tell us about what actually is so, although it might have been otherwise. Scientists must make observations and conduct experiments in order to know whether the sentences are true.

In pure mathematics, however, and in logic, we do not have to employ observations or experiments. The sentences in which the principles of mathematics and logic are expressed are a priori necessary sentences (for example, "$x + y = y + x$" and "If no F's are G's then no G's are F's"). The principles of mathematics and logic give us no specific information about this particular world that happens to exist, but apply equally to all conceivable worlds. Such of these principles as we attain knowledge of, we can know by means of reflection without appeal to sense experience.

Second, a practical reason why the distinction between necessary and empirical sentences is worth noticing is that it can help us to evaluate sentences met in ordinary discourse. Sometimes a person wishes to assert an informative, empirical thought, but without realizing the difference the speaker asserts something necessarily true but trivial instead. For example, perhaps the speaker comes out in ringing tones with the declaration "The future lies before us"; the speaker imagines that this is an important insight. But when you stop to think about it, you can see that there is nowhere the future could lie except before us—the remark is a necessary truth, and it does not convey any interesting information. Listeners may give the wrong weight to what was said and may ask for the wrong kinds of reasons in its support, if they do not notice that the sentence is necessarily true rather than empirical. Also, speakers sometimes utter necessarily false sentences without realizing that they are doing so. "Phyllis is younger than Joanna, Joanna is younger than Sybil, and Sybil is younger than Phyllis," someone may say, thinking that this is just a description of the facts. But of course it is an impossible description; this is necessarily false. Here too listeners will give the wrong weight to what is said and may try in the wrong way to evaluate it, if they do not notice the necessary falsehood of the remark.

Of course, trying to distinguish between empirical and necessary sentences brings us face to face with problems about the language we speak. One problem is that many words in our language are *vague*: it is unsettled just where correct use of a word begins and where it leaves off, as things vary in degree. For instance, the word "bald" is vague, for baldness is a matter of degree, and we cannot say just how many hairs must be missing before it is correct to describe a person as bald; there is a 'gray area' between being bald and not being bald. Vagueness on the part of the words a sentence contains can sometimes make for vagueness about whether that sentence is empirical or necessary—for example, the sentence "Bald men have little hair on their heads" is impossible to classify definitely as empirical or as necessary because it contains two quite vague words, "bald" and "little." If by "bald men" were meant "totally bald men," then the sentence would be necessarily true; but if by "bald men" were meant "men at least slightly bald," then the sentence would be empirical and false. So vagueness can cause trouble here.

Another problem is that many words in our language are *ambiguous*: they have two or more different meanings. For instance, the word "heavy" in the sentence "This is a heavy book" is ambiguous, for it may have either of two quite different meanings: "hard to read" or "hard to lift." Ambiguity can make it difficult to tell whether a sentence is empirical or necessary. Thus, "Heavy books are massive" would be a necessary truth if "heavy" means "hard to lift," but would be empirical if "heavy" means "hard to read." In cases like this it is necessary to determine which meaning is intended for the ambiguous word before the sentence can be classified.

Some people who study logic form the mistaken impression that vagueness and ambiguity are always bad features for language to have, and they imagine that ideally we ought to use words that have no vagueness or ambiguity. This is a wrong idea. It would be impossible to eliminate all vagueness and ambiguity from our language. In any case, it would be undesirable to do so; often we want to speak vaguely or ambiguously, and we need language that permits this. What we should do is to become aware of the vagueness and ambiguity in our language, so that in particular cases where these features might cause trouble we can be armed against it. (There will be further discussion of ambiguity in Chapter 5.)

EXERCISE 3

*A When each sentence is straightforwardly understood, does it say something necessarily true, necessarily false, or empirical? If more than one answer is possible, explain the alternative interpretations.

1 Some roses are red.
2 All roses are flowers.
3 There are no living organisms on the Moon.
4 Whatever will be, will be.
5 Penguins are not the only birds to be found in Antarctica.
6 Either Sheila is my friend, or she is not my friend.
7 Either Sheila is my friend, or she's my enemy.
8 If no Hindus are Buddhists, then no Buddhists are Hindus.
9 Every cube has twelve edges.
10 Some cubes have fewer than twelve edges.
11 No bishops are generals.
12 Some whole numbers are not divisible by one.

B Same instructions as for part A.
1 The centerfielder leaped in vain for McGurk's towering drive; luckily it was foul by inches.
2 Every electron has a negative charge.
3 We were incorrect in stating that Halifax is farther north than Edmonton. In fact, Edmonton is south of Halifax.
4 If you eat an adequate, well-balanced diet, you will get all the vitamins your body normally needs.
5 All the matter in the universe is made up of chemical elements.
6 Turn on the pressure and the good guys always come through.
7 Crocker Corporation increased its earnings during each quarter of the year just ended. However, the gains were not sufficient to bring the corporation's earnings for the full year up to the level of the preceding year.
8 Radioactive cesium produces dangerous radiation. Although it takes thirty years for half of it to decay harmlessly, the material is gradually excreted from the body so that most of it is gone after a year.
9 It is not wholesome for a person to spend too much time thinking unduly morbid thoughts.
10 No thinker can get outside his own world of thought.
11 The tiny island nations of Lichtenburg and Luxenstein have a long history of border skirmishes.
12 No statement is wholly true.

C In each case, if your answer is yes, give an example to establish your answer. If your answer is no, explain why there can be no example.
1 Can there be a valid deductive argument consisting entirely of empirical sentences?
2 Can there be a valid deductive argument consisting entirely of necessary sentences?
3 Consider a valid deductive argument all of whose premises are necessarily true. Can its conclusion be an empirical sentence?
4 Consider a valid deductive argument all of whose premises are true empirical sentences. Can its conclusion be a necessary sentence?
5 Consider a valid deductive argument all of whose premises are false empirical sentences. Can its conclusion be a necessary sentence?

D In logic it is important to distinguish between what necessarily follows from a remark and what is merely suggested by it. In each case, suppose someone says (a). Then is (b) something that follows as a valid deductive conclusion?

1 (a) Only friends of mine are invited to my party.
(b) Every friend of mine is invited to my party.

2 (a) All of them who like dancing like music.
(b) All of them who don't like music don't like dancing.

3 (a) Madrid is farther north than Washington.
(b) Washington is farther south than Madrid.

4 (a) Boy Scouts are as clean as they are reverent.
(b) Boy Scouts are clean and reverent.

5 (a) If you buy now, you'll get a low price.
(b) If you don't buy now, you won't get a low price.

6 (a) The club is open to anyone who is a member or a guest.
(b) The club is open to anyone who is both a member and a guest.

7 (a) Only buses are permitted in the right lane.
(b) Buses are permitted only in the right lane.

8 (a) Carelessly, he anchored in the target area.
(b) He anchored carelessly in the target area.

9 (a) Some of her dogs are well trained.
(b) Some of her dogs are not well trained.

10 (a) Each human action aims at a goal.
(b) There is a goal at which all human actions aim.

CHAPTER 2

THE LOGIC OF CATEGORICAL SENTENCES

In this chapter we shall study a traditional part of logic which was first worked out by Aristotle, and which logicians in medieval and early modern times regarded as the most important part of logic, or even as the whole of it. Nowadays we see that such a view is far too narrow; many important forms of argument are not included within this traditional part of logic. Nevertheless, this part of logic is well worth studying. The arguments that it does deal with occur frequently in ordinary thinking, they can be analyzed without much use of symbols, and they form a systematic body of traditional doctrine.

4 CATEGORICAL SENTENCES

Our approach will be to study certain standard forms of sentences, getting clear about the logical relations among them. After that, we shall see that the logical relations among many other sentences can also be clarified, because these other sentences can be translated into our standard forms.

The Four Categorical Forms

Let us focus our attention upon four specific forms of sentence, forms important enough so that they were long ago given the special names "**A**," "**E**," "**I**," and "**O**." These four forms of sentence are:

    A: All so-and-so's are such-and-such's.

E: No so-and-so's are such-and-such's.
I: Some so-and-so's are such-and-such's.
O: Some so-and-so's are not such-and-such's.

Sentences of these four forms, and only these, we shall call *categorical* sentences.[8] Thus, for example, the sentence "All unicorns are animals" is a categorical sentence of the **A** form; the sentence "No natural satellites of the earth are self-luminous bodies" is a categorical sentence of the **E** form; the sentence "Some philosophers are theists" is a sentence of the **I** form; and the sentence "Some birds are not dodoes" is a categorical sentence of the **O** form.

To be in categorical form, a sentence must start with a *quantifier* (the word "all," "no," or "some"), followed by the word or phrase called the *subject* of the sentence, then the *copula* ("are" or "are not"), and finally the word or phrase called the *predicate* (Figure 1). The words or phrases that serve as subjects and predicates in categorical sentences are called *terms*.

Our consideration of categorical sentences will be smoother and clearer if we adhere to this strict and narrow point of view concerning the forms they have. (This will facilitate our discussion of immediate inference, later on, when we shall talk about letting the subject and predicate trade places.) Accordingly, let us insist that in a sentence strictly in categorical form the copula must be plural and the terms must be plural substantive general terms.[9] Thus, the sentence "All gold is valuable" is not strictly in categorical form, because its copula is "is" rather than "are" and because its predicate is an adjective rather than a substantive (a nounlike expression). However, if we reword it as "All pieces of gold are valuable things," then we have a sentence that is strictly categorical.

The **A** and **E** sentences are said to be *universal*, because sentences of these forms sweepingly speak of the whole of the class of things to which the subject term applies. The **I** and **O** forms are said to be *particular*, because sentences of these forms give definite information only about part of the class of things to which the subject term applies. This is called *quantity*. **A** and **E** are said to be universal in quantity, while **I** and **O** are said to be particular in quantity.

The **A** and **I** forms say something *affirmative*, while **E** and **O** say something *negative*. This is called *quality*. **A** and **I** are said to be affirmative in quality, while **I** and **O** are said to be negative in quality. (The four letters used as names

Figure 1

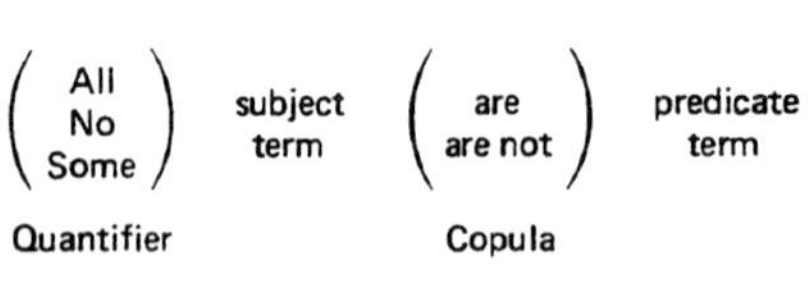

Categorical Sentence

$$\left(\begin{array}{c} \text{All} \\ \text{No} \\ \text{Some} \end{array} \right) \quad \begin{array}{c} \text{subject} \\ \text{term} \end{array} \quad \left(\begin{array}{c} \text{are} \\ \text{are not} \end{array} \right) \quad \begin{array}{c} \text{predicate} \\ \text{term} \end{array}$$

Quantifier   Copula

of these forms come from the vowels in the Latin words "**affirmo**"—"I affirm"—and "**nego**"—"I deny." In medieval and early modern times, logic, like all university subjects, was studied in Latin.) We can use a little diagram to sum up these facts about quantity and quality (Figure 2).

Before we can discuss categorical sentences further, we need to face two sorts of ambiguity that affect our use of the word "some." First, the word "some" is vague as it is ordinarily used. By "some" we mean "a few"; but how many are a few? If a person says that some chairs are in the next room, is the person claiming that there is at least one chair in the next room, that there are at least two, or what? Such questions have no answer, for the word "some" is vague as ordinarily used. Vagueness of this sort is inconvenient for our present purposes. It will be best for us to assign a definite meaning to the word "some." The most convenient way to do this is to assign it the minimum meaning: We shall stipulate that "Some so-and-so's are such-and-such's" is to mean that there is *at least one* so-and-so that is a such-and-such.

A second difficulty is that the word "some" can give rise to ambiguity as it is ordinarily used. Consider a person who states that some men are boring. Is the speaker thereby claiming that some men are *not* boring? In ordinary discourse this occasionally may be part of what such a remark means, although more often it is not. For example, a student who says in an acid tone "Some teachers are worth listening to" is strongly suggesting that some are not, and perhaps we should regard his remark as asserting that some are and some are not worth listening to. But usually to say that some so-and-so's are such-and-such's is to leave it an open question whether some are not.

For the purposes of logic, it is best to choose the minimum meaning of "some." We shall interpret sentences of the form "Some so-and-so's are such-and-such's" as meaning merely that there is at least one so-and-so that is a such-and-such, and leaving it entirely open whether there is any so-and-so that is not a such-and-such. Similarly, we shall interpret the **O** sentence

Figure 2

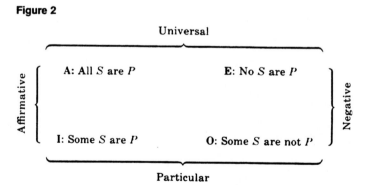

as meaning merely that at least one so-and-so is not a such-and-such, leaving it an open question whether any is.

Venn Diagrams

We can understand the meanings of the four forms of categorical sentences especially clearly if we picture them by means of a kind of diagram devised by the nineteenth-century English logician John Venn.

Let us draw two overlapping circles (Figure 3) and consider two classes of individuals, Swedes and Protestants. We shall now imagine that all the Swedes there are are herded inside the left-hand circle; no one else and nothing else may enter. Into the right-hand circle all Protestants are herded; no one else and nothing else is allowed in that circle. In region 1 of the diagram we now shall find Swedes who are not Protestants, if there are any. In region 2 we would find Swedes who are Protestants. In region 3 of the diagram we would find Protestants who are not Swedes. And in region 4 will be all persons and things that are neither Swedes nor Protestants.

Now consider the I sentence "Some Swedes are Protestants." At present we are not concerned with whether this sentence is true or false, but only with what it means. Let us try to draw a diagram indicating exactly what the sentence says, no more and no less. To do this, we put an asterisk in region 2 to indicate that this region is not empty (Figure 4). This diagram indicates that region 2 is occupied by at least one thing, and so it exhibits exactly the information conveyed by the I sentence. All other regions remain blank, indicating that the I sentence tells us nothing about whether they are vacant or occupied.

Using the same method, we can illustrate what the O sentence says (Figure 5). Here the asterisk in region 1 means that there is at least one thing that is an S but not a P.

Diagrams also can be drawn for the universal sentences. Here we shade a region to indicate that it is empty. The A sentence says in effect that there are no S's that fail to be P's, and so we shade region 1 (Figure 6). The E sentence says that there are no S's that are P's, and so we shade region 2 (Figure 7). Notice that as we are interpreting them neither of these universal sentences implies the existence of anything.

Distribution of Terms

In medieval logic, some of the terms occurring in categorical sentences were said to be "distributed," and others were said to be "undistributed." Tradi-

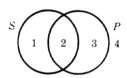

Figure 3

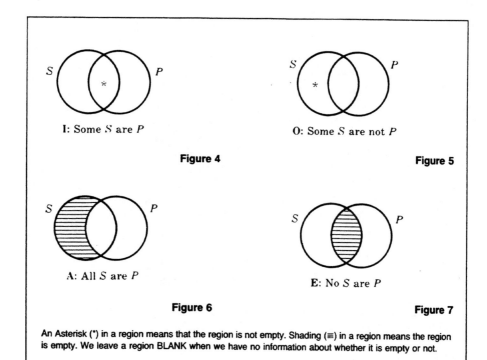

I: Some S are P

Figure 4

O: Some S are not P

Figure 5

A: All S are P

Figure 6

E: No S are P

Figure 7

An Asterisk (*) in a region means that the region is not empty. Shading (≡) in a region means the region is empty. We leave a region BLANK when we have no information about whether it is empty or not.

tional definitions of this notion of distribution were rather unsatisfactory, but the notion is a useful one, as we shall see later on. Let us redefine it as follows: A term S occurring as the subject of a categorical sentence is said to be *distributed* in that sentence just in case the sentence, in virtue of its form, says something about *every kind of* S. Similarly, a term P occurring as the predicate of a categorical sentence is said to be distributed in that sentence just in case the sentence, in virtue of its form, says something about *every kind of* P.

Consider the sentence "All scholars are pedants." Again, we are not concerned with whether this is true, but only with what it means. The sentence says something about every kind of scholar: young ones, old ones, rich ones, poor ones. It says that all kinds of scholars are pedants. However, the sentence does not say something about every kind of pedant; it concerns only ones who are scholars and tells us nothing about pedants who may not be scholars. Thus, in this **A** sentence the subject term is distributed, while the predicate term is undistributed.

Consider next the sentence "No scholars are pedants." Here again our sentence says something about every kind of scholar; it says, of large ones, small ones, fat ones, slim ones, that none of them is a pedant. And, though more indirectly, it says something about all kinds of pedants: whether happy or sad, wise or foolish, it tells us that none of them is a scholar. Thus both the subject and predicate of this **E** sentence are distributed.

Now consider the sentence "Some scholars are pedants." This sentence does not say anything about every kind of scholar; it speaks only about those of them who are pedants. Neither does it say anything about every kind of pedant; it speaks only about those of them who are scholars. Thus in this **I** sentence, neither the subject nor the predicate is distributed.

Finally, consider the sentence "Some scholars are not pedants." Here again nothing is said about every kind of scholar. However, in a roundabout way, a claim is made concerning every kind of pedant. For this **O** sentence says that whatever kind of pedant you consider, sane ones, mad ones, tall ones, short ones, each of these kinds of pedants is not such as to include all scholars. That is, our original sentence implies that some scholars are not sane pedants, that some scholars are not mad pedants, and so on. Thus in the **O** sentence the subject is undistributed but the predicate is distributed.

What has been said about these sample sentences holds true in general. In any **A** sentence the subject is distributed but the predicate is undistributed; in any **E** sentence both subject and predicate are distributed; in any **I** sentence neither subject nor predicate is distributed; and in any **O** sentence the subject is undistributed but the predicate is distributed.

One way of remembering these facts is to remember that in any universal sentence the subject is distributed, while in any negative sentence the predicate is distributed. Another way of remembering them is to use the mnemonic word "AsEbInOp," which means that in **A** the subject is distributed, in **E** both subject and predicate, in **I** neither, and in **O** the predicate.[10]

EXERCISE 4

*A Which sentences are in categorical form just as they stand? For those that are, name the form, say what the quantity and quality are, draw the Venn diagram, and say which terms are distributed.

1 No Shawnees are Iroquois.
2 Some ancient Romans were Christians.
3 All igneous rocks are volcanic.
4 Some snakes are not vipers.
5 No leukocytes are phagocytes.
6 All Australia is a continent.
7 Some contestants will be big winners.
8 All sonnets are poems.
9 All toads are not frogs.
10 Some trespassers will be welcome guests.
11 An elephant is a pachyderm.
12 Some real numbers are not rational numbers.
13 All scientific theories are contributions to knowledge.
14 Few people are permanent residents of Greenland.
15 No alleged cases of precognition are phenomena that have actually occurred.
16 Some accountants are highly trained professionals.
17 All things she likes are things he likes.
18 Every blue whale eats tons of tiny animals each day.

19 Some steamships are driven by turbines.
20 Whoever likes Tchaikovsky likes Brahms.
21 No murderers are guiltless.
22 No guerrillas are regular soldiers.
23 All crimes shall be reported to the authorities.
24 Some vegetables are not nutritious foods.
25 There are some carnivorous reptiles.

B Draw a Venn diagram for each of the following sentences. First do so using circles labeled "non-Ontarians" and "non-Canadians". Then do so using circles labeled "Ontarians" and "Canadians".

1 All non-Canadians are non-Ontarians.
2 No non-Canadians are non-Ontarians.
3 Some non-Canadians are non-Ontarians.
4 Some non-Canadians are not non-Ontarians.
5 All non-Ontarians are non-Canadians.
6 No non-Ontarians are non-Canadians.
7 Some non-Ontarians are non-Canadians.
8 Some non-Ontarians are not non-Canadians.

5 THE SQUARE OF OPPOSITION

Suppose that we have categorical sentences of different forms but with the same subject and the same predicate: "All S are P," "No S are P," and "Some S are P," "Some S are not P." What logical relations will hold among them? Before we can answer this question in any particular case, we first must decide from what viewpoint the relations among these **A**, **E**, **I**, and **O** sentences are to be discussed. As we discuss these relations, are we keeping open the possibility that there are no S's, or are we excluding that possibility by presupposing that there is at least one S? It makes a difference.

If we consider the logical relations among these categorical sentences from a viewpoint which presupposes that there exist things of some specified kind, then we are adopting what we shall call an *existential viewpoint*. If we consider the relation among these categorical sentences without taking for granted that any things exist, then we are adopting what we shall call the *hypothetical viewpoint*. Of course there could be intermediate existential viewpoints where we take for granted the existence of some of the kinds of things under discussion but not others. However, for our present purposes, the question is whether to presuppose that there exists at least one thing to which the subject term, S, applies.

First let us consider how the four categorical forms are related to one another if we do not presuppose the existence of S's (or of anything else). Let us consider the logical relations among the sentences "All succubi are poltergeists," "No succubi are poltergeists," "Some succubi are poltergeists," and "Some succubi are not poltergeists." Here we shall keep open the possibility that succubi may not exist. The relationships can be exhibited in a diagram that is called the square of opposition (Figure 8).

As the Venn diagrams show, **A** (which says that all succubi are polter-

Square of Opposition

Hypothetical viewpoint: We do
not presuppose that any S exists.

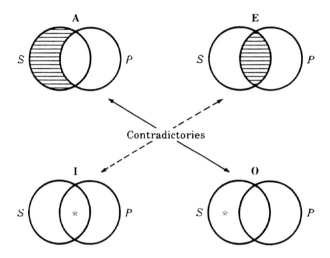

Contradictories

Figure 8

geists) and **O** (which says that some succubi are not poltergeists) are oppo-site as regards their truth or falsity. **A** says exactly what **O** denies, no less and no more. **A** and **O** are called *contradictories* of each other. **E** and **I** are also contradictories, for what **E** says ("No succubi are poltergeists") is ex-actly what **I** denies ("Some succubi are poltergeists"), no less and no more.

Is **A** related to **I**? You might have thought that **A** ("All succubi are pol-tergeists") would imply **I** ("Some succubi are poltergeists"). But this is not so. The truth of **A** does not guarantee the truth of **I**, for it is possible that **A** might be true and **I** false—this will happen if there are no succubi. Then **I** is false (when there are no succubi, it is false that some of them are polter-geists), while **A** is true (when there are no succubi, it will be true that none of them fail to be poltergeists—which is what **A** means). There is no logical connection between **A** and **I**; knowledge of the truth or falsity of one of these sentences does not enable us to tell whether the other is true or whether it is false.

Similarly, **E** ("No succubi are poltergeists") does not imply **O** ("Some succubi are not poltergeists"), for **E** could be true if **O** is false. This will hap-pen if S's do not exist. In that case it will be true that no S are P but false that some S are not P. There is no logical connection between **E** and **O**.

Is **A** ("All succubi are poltergeists") related to **E** ("No succubi are polter-geists")? You might have thought that it would be impossible for them both to be true, but this is not so. These sentences will both be true if there are no succubi (S's) at all. When nothing is an S, certainly nothing is an S that fails to be P, and also there are no S that are P. So the **A** and **E** sentences will both be true. Thus there is no logical connection between **A** and **E**; knowing the truth or falsity of one of them does not enable us to tell the truth or falsity of the other.

How about **I** ("Some succubi are poltergeists") and **O** ("Some succubi are not poltergeists")? You might have thought that they cannot both be false, but it is not so either. **I** says that there is at least one S that is P, while **O** says that there is at least one S that is not P; both these sentences will be false if there are no S's at all. Thus there is no logical connection between **I** and **O**.

Now let us consider the matter again, but this time from an existential viewpoint rather than from the hypothetical viewpoint. Let us consider the four sentences "All Samoans are pantheists," "No Samoans are pantheists," "Some Samoans are pantheists," and "Some Samoans are not pantheists." We want to know how these sentences are related, under the presupposition that there are Samoans. Our results will be brought together in Figure 9.

If it is true that all Samoans are pantheists, then (since we take for

Figure 9

Square of Opposition

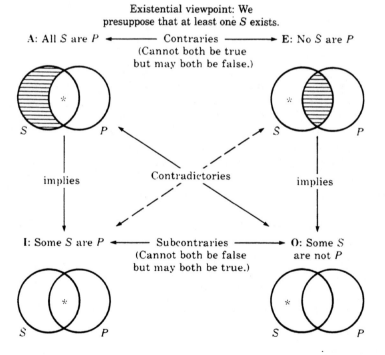

Existential viewpoint: We presuppose that at least one S exists.

A: All S are P ← ——— Contraries ——— → E: No S are P
(Cannot both be true
but may both be false.)

implies · · · Contradictories · · · implies

I: Some S are P ← ——— Subcontraries ——— → O: Some S are not P
(Cannot both be false
but may both be true.)

granted that there are Samoans) it must be true that some Samoans are pantheists. Thus the truth of the **A** sentence will guarantee the truth of the **I**, and in this sense **A** implies **I**. On the other hand, that some Samoans are pantheists does not guarantee that all of them are (since some might be and some not). Thus we can fully describe the relation between **A** and **I** by saying that **A** implies **I** but **I** does not imply **A**.

Similarly, if it is true that no Samoans are pantheists, then (since we take for granted that there are Samoans) it must follow that some Samoans are not pantheists. Thus the **E** sentence implies the **O**. However, that some Samoans are not pantheists does not guarantee that no Samoans are (for perhaps some of them are and some are not). Thus we can describe the relation between **E** and **O** by saying that **E** implies **O** but **O** does not imply **E**.

As for **A** and **E**, neither implies the other. But if we take for granted that there are Samoans, it cannot be true both that all Samoans are pantheists and that no Samoans are pantheists; that is, **A** and **E** cannot both be true. Might **A** and **E** both be false? Yes, for if some Samoans are pantheists and some are not, then neither **A** nor **E** is true. Thus the relation between **A** and **E** is that they cannot both be true but they may both be false. The traditional way of referring to this relationship is to call **A** and **E** *contrary* sentences.

The relationship between **I** and **O** is somewhat similar. Neither implies the other. Both may be true. But if we take for granted that Samoans exist, then **I** and **O** cannot both be false; if there are Samoans, as we are assuming, then either some of them are pantheists or some of them are not pantheists (or perhaps both). Thus **I** and **O** are related in such a way that they cannot both be false, although they may both be true. The traditional way of referring to this relationship is to call **I** and **O** *subcontraries*.

Now consider the relationship between **A** and **O**. If it is true that all Samoans are pantheists, it must be false that some of them are not pantheists. And if it is false that all Samoans are pantheists, then it must be true that some of them are not. Conversely, if it is true that some Samoans are not pantheists, it must be false that all Samoans are; and if it is false that some Samoans are not pantheists, then it must be true that all of them are. Thus **A** and **O** cannot both be true, and they cannot both be false; they are opposite as regards truth and falsity. They are called *contradictories* of each other.

Similarly, **E** and **I** are related in such a way that if **E** is true, **I** must be false, and if **E** is false, then **I** must be true. **E** and **I** are always opposite as regards truth and falsity, and so they too are contradictories of each other.

These relationships can be displayed in a diagram for the square of opposition under an existential interpretation (Figure 9).[11] Here each of the four Venn diagrams contains an asterisk, because we are presupposing throughout that at least one S exists.

We have now discussed the square of opposition both from the hypothetical viewpoint and from an existential viewpoint. Which viewpoint should we adopt when we are studying an actual example? We ought to choose whichever viewpoint makes the best sense of the remarks we are studying.

Here we need to consider the circumstances under which the remarks are made. Sometimes the hypothetical viewpoint is definitely called for, but often an existential viewpoint is more appropriate. Let us consider an example of each situation.

Suppose that a landowner has said "All trespassers are people who will be prosecuted." We wonder about the logical relation of this remark to the sentence "Some trespassers are people who will be prosecuted." Does believing the former sentence commit the landowner to believing the latter sentence also? Here our answer must depend on whether the possibility is left open that perhaps no one trespasses. In this example it is better to regard that possibility as indeed left open, and therefore our answer should be that it does not follow. There are two reasons for preferring the hypothetical interpretation here. First, the landowner, in speaking that way, may have hoped that the remark would serve as an effective warning, preventing all trespassing. Second, the possibility that there may be no trespassers is a reasonable sort of possibility; so far as we know, not all lands get trespassed upon.

On the other hand, suppose a woman says "All my jewels are diamonds." Is she committed to the consequence "Some of my jewels are diamonds"? Here it would be inappropriate to say that perhaps she has no jewels and so it does not follow. Such a response would not make good sense in this case. By speaking as she did, the woman indicated that she believes she owns jewels, and she should know what she owns. The sensible thing for us to do is to adopt an existential viewpoint and carry on our discussion presupposing that she does have jewels. So the best answer would be that the **I** sentence does follow from the **A** in this example.

Traditional aristotelian logic considered sentences only from an existential viewpoint. Modern symbolic logic usually treats them only from the hypothetical viewpoint. But the best approach is to understand both viewpoints and to be able to use whichever one is more appropriate to a particular case. Of course it can sometimes happen that one encounters a case where the two viewpoints give different answers, and yet neither viewpoint is clearly preferable to the other or more fair to what the speakers are trying to say. Then there is no definitely right answer, and the best we can do is to recognize what the situation is and why it is ambiguous.

EXERCISE 5

*A In each case: (a) Suppose the first sentence is true; what can you tell about the second? (b) Suppose the first sentence is false; what can you tell about the second? (c) Suppose the second sentence is true, what can you tell about the first? (d) Suppose the second sentence is false, what can you tell about the first? Answer first from an existential viewpoint, and then answer from the hypothetical viewpoint.

    1 All frigates are warships. Some frigates are not warships.
    2 Some pantheists are Marxists. No pantheists are Marxists.

 3 All Rumanians are Slavs. No Rumanians are Slavs.
 4 No pharmacists are realtors. Some pharmacists are not realtors.
 5 Some novels are romances. Some novels are not romances.
 6 All pines are softwoods. Some pines are softwoods.
 7 Some mammals are not land creatures. All mammals are land creatures.
 8 No centaurs are nymphs. Some centaurs are nymphs.
 9 Some sailors are not puritans. No sailors are puritans.
 10 No merchants are saints. All merchants are saints.
 11 Some oranges are not seedless fruits. Some oranges are seedless fruits.
 12 Some commodities are poor investments. All commodities are poor investments.

B For each example, discuss whether an existential interpretation or the hypothetical interpretation is more appropriate.

 1 The preacher declares that no true Christians in the congregation are persons who envy others. Should this be understood as logically implying that some true Christians in the congregation are not persons who envy others?

 2 The Watusi chieftain boasts that all sons of his are persons more than 7 feet tall. Does this logically imply that some sons of his are persons more than 7 feet tall?

 3 The physics book states that all ideal gases are such that PV equals RT. If this is so, must it be false that no ideal gases are such that PV equals RT?

 4 A biologist says it is false that some Loch Ness monsters are reptiles. Does this imply that some Loch Ness monsters are not reptiles?

 5 A teacher says it is false that some of her fellow teachers are not pushers of dope. Does this imply the falsity of the statement that no fellow teachers of hers are pushers of dope?

 6 A union leader says it is false that some corporations are payers of fair wages. Does this imply the falsity of the statement that all corporations are payers of fair wages?

 7 An engineer asserts that no bridges he has designed are unstable structures. Does this imply the falsity of the statement that all bridges he has designed are unstable structures?

 8 A politician says it is false that some times when he has been offered bribes are times when he has accepted them. Does this imply that some times when he has been offered bribes are not times when he has accepted them?

6 OPERATIONS ON CATEGORICAL SENTENCES

Next we shall consider several basic operations that we can perform on categorical sentences. These are ways of changing around categorical sentences so as to produce new ones. For each type of case, we shall want to notice how the new sentence and the original are logically related. In certain cases we shall find that one can validly be inferred from the other. Traditionally, these relationships were studied under the title of "immediate inferences"—inferences where only one premise directly yields the conclusion. In discussing these relationships we do not need to worry about any contrast between hypothetical and existential viewpoints except when we come to conversion by limitation; only there will it make any difference.

Conversion

A simple way to alter a categorical sentence is to make the subject and predicate trade places. This is *conversion*, and the new sentence obtained by this operation is called the *converse* of the original sentence. (It is sometimes called the *simple* converse, to contrast it with the converse by limitation, which will be discussed presently.) Let us consider how the meanings of the various forms of categorical sentence are affected by conversion.

Suppose we start with the **E** sentence "No Spaniards are Portuguese." When subject and predicate trade places, we get the converse "No Portuguese are Spaniards." A pair of Venn diagrams drawn from the hypothetical viewpoint (Figure 10) can help us to see how the original and its converse are related. Two sentences are said to be *equivalent* if they are necessarily alike as regards truth and falsity. Here the diagrams are just the same, showing that the **E** sentence and its converse are equivalent. Thus it is valid to infer either one from the other. Notice that a pair of Venn diagrams drawn from an existential viewpoint (putting an asterisk in the S region of each diagram) would give us the same result: both sentences are alike in their diagrams, from either viewpoint.

The **I** sentence "Some Sudanese are pagans" has as its converse the sentence "Some pagans are Sudanese." Here again it is clear that conversion has left the meaning of the sentence basically unchanged; the **I** and its con-

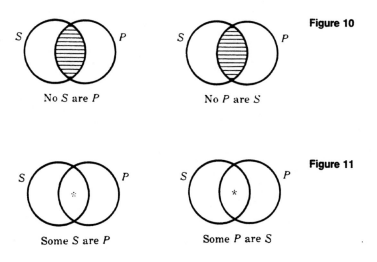

Figure 10

No S are P   No P are S

Figure 11

Some S are P   Some P are S

verse are equivalent, as the diagrams show (Figure 11). Either may be inferred from the other.

Next consider the **A** sentence "All sunflowers are plants." When subject and predicate trade places, we obtain the converse "All plants are sunflowers." How is the new sentence related to the original one? From the diagram (Figure 12) it is clear that the new sentence says something completely different from what our original sentence said. They are logically independent. So of course they are not equivalent, and neither can be inferred from the other.

Finally, if we convert the **O** sentence "Some soldiers are not patriots," we obtain "Some patriots are not soldiers." Here too it is clear from the diagram (Figure 13) that the original sentence and its converse are logically independent of one another.

What holds good in these examples holds in general. We can sum up by saying that any **E** or **I** sentence is equivalent to its converse, while any **A** or **O** sentence is logically independent of its converse. Another way of describing the matter is to say that when subject and predicate in the original sentence are alike as regards distribution (either both distributed or both undistributed), then the converse will be equivalent to the original sentence; but when the subject and predicate in the original sentence differ as regards distribution, then the converse will not be equivalent to the original sentence.

Conversion by Limitation

Although an **A** sentence is not equivalent to its simple converse, we can validly derive from the **A** sentence another sentence in which subject and

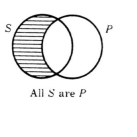
All S are P

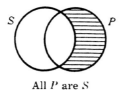
All P are S

Figure 12

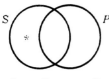

Some S are not P

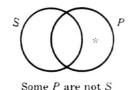
Some P are not S

Figure 13

predicate have changed places. This is a sort of substitute for a simple converse, and it is called the *converse by limitation* (or the converse per *accidens*). This new sentence will be an **I**. From "All sows are pigs" we may validly infer "Some pigs are sows." This inference is legitimate only from an existential viewpoint; it is the existence of sows that must be presupposed here. Moreover, the converse by limitation is merely implied by the original sentence; it is of course not equivalent to it (Figure 14).

Obversion

The operation of conversion has the disadvantage that only sometimes is the converse equivalent to the original sentence. Obversion is an operation free from this disadvantage. However, it involves a slightly more complicated alteration. To form the obverse of a categorical sentence we do two things: we change the quality of the sentence, and we negate the predicate term as a whole.

Suppose we start with the **A** sentence "All saints are puritans." This is a universal affirmative, and so to change its quality we must turn it into a negative sentence. We leave the quantity unaltered. Thus we shall obtain a universal negative sentence, that is, a sentence of the **E** form. Also, we are to negate the predicate, replacing the term "puritans" by "nonpuritans." We leave the subject unaltered. As a result of these two steps we obtain the new sentence "No saints are nonpuritans," which is the obverse of our original sentence. Here we can see (Figure 15) that the **A** sentence and its obverse are equivalent.

If we start with the **E** sentence "No Syrians are Persians," we form its obverse by changing the quality from negative to affirmative and by negating

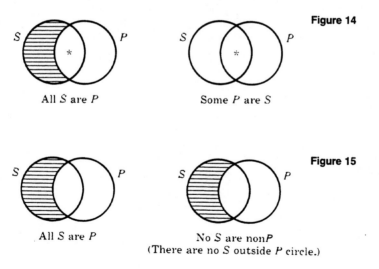

Figure 14

All S are P Some P are S

Figure 15

All S are P No S are non$P$
(There are no S outside P circle.)

the predicate. Thus we obtain the obverse "All Syrians are non-Persians." Here again we can see from the diagrams (Figure 16) that the original sentence and its obverse are equivalent.

If we start with the **I** sentence "Some shells are projectiles," we form its obverse by changing it from particular affirmative to particular negative and by negating the predicate. We obtain "Some shells are not nonprojectiles." It is clear (Figure 17) that this is equivalent to our original sentence.

Finally, if we begin with the **O** sentence "Some Senegalese are not pygmies," we change from particular negative to particular affirmative and negate the predicate, thus obtaining the obverse "Some Senegalese are nonpygmies." In this case the obverse is so very similar to the original sentence that it almost looks as though no change had taken place. But a change has occurred, for we consider the obverse to be in **I** form and to have the negation as part of its predicate, while the original is in **O** form and has the negation as part of its copula. When we write such sentences, it will help to avoid confusion if so far as possible we use "non" to express negation that belongs to the term and reserve "not" to express negation that is part of the copula.

Contraposition

Suppose we start with an **A** sentence "All *S* are *P*" and obvert it into "No *S* are non*P*," then convert that into "No non*P* are *S*," and finally obvert that to "All non*P* are non*S*." These steps are performed in such a way that each new sentence is equivalent to the previous one. The final result is equivalent to the original, and it is related to the original in a way interesting enough to have a special name. "All non*P* are non*S*" is called the *contrapositive* of "All *S* are *P*." A briefer way of describing how the contrapositive is obtained is to say that the subject and predicate of the original trade places and each is negated. As we see, with the **A** form, the contrapositive is equivalent to the original.

With the **E** form, this process of obverting, converting, and then obverting again runs into difficulty. The second step would involve converting an **A**

Figure 16

No *S* are *P*

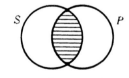

All *S* are non*P*
(All *S* are outside *P* circle.)

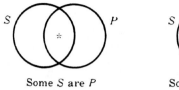 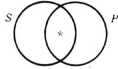

Some S are P   Some S are not nonP
(Some S are not outside P circle.)

Figure 17

sentence, and an **A** is not equivalent to its converse. If the original **E** sentence were "No S are P," its contrapositive would be "No nonP are nonS"; however, this is not equivalent to the original.

If we start with an **I** sentence, obvert it, and then convert it and obvert it again, we would likewise encounter difficulty. In this case the second step would involve converting an **O** sentence, and the **O** is not equivalent to its converse. Thus the **I** sentence "Some S are P" is not equivalent to its contrapositive "Some nonP are nonS."

However, if we start with an **O** sentence, we can obvert, convert, and obvert again without difficulty. The **O** sentence "Some S are not P" is equivalent to its contrapositive "Some nonP are not nonS."

Summary

Thus we see that while conversion is always permissible with **E** and **I** but not with **A** and **O**, contraposition is always permissible with **A** and **O** but not with **E** and **I**. We may sum up as follows the relationships that have just been discussed.

Conversion (No existential presupposition needed)
"No S are P" is equivalent to "No P are S."
"Some S are P" is equivalent to "Some P are S."

Conversion by limitation (Must presuppose that there are S 's)
"All S are P" implies "Some P are S."

Obversion (No existential presupposition needed)
"All S are P" is equivalent to "No S are nonP."
"No S are P" is equivalent to "All S are nonP."
"Some S are P" is equivalent to "Some S are not nonP."
"Some S are not P" is equivalent to "Some S are nonP."

Contraposition (No existential presupposition needed)
"All S are P" is equivalent to "All nonP are nonS."
"Some S are not P" is equivalent to "Some nonP are not nonS."

Symmetry of These Relations

It is worth noticing that the relation between any categorical sentence and its converse is a symmetrical relation. That is, if the sentence r is the converse of the sentence q, then q is the converse of r. In other words, if we obtain r by transposing the subject and predicate of q, then were we to start with r and transpose its subject and predicate, the result would be q.

Similarly, the relation between any categorical sentence and its obverse is in effect a symmetrical relation. If r is the obverse of q, then q must be equivalent to the obverse of r. For example, if q is "All S are P," its obverse r is "No S are nonP." What is the obverse of r? If we change the quality and negate the predicate of r, we get "All S are non-nonP," and letting the double negative in the predicate cancel out, we have "All S are P," which is q. Notice that this sort of double negation may be canceled out, because any categorical sentence containing a doubly negated term always is equivalent to an otherwise similar sentence with the negations canceled out. But we must beware of supposing that two negatives of different types always cancel each other. For example, "No nonS are P" is definitely not equivalent to "All S are P" (think of "All chows are dogs" and "No nonchows are dogs"— one is true and the other is false, and so it is clear that they are not equivalent).

Also, the relation between a sentence and its contrapositive is in effect symmetrical. If r is the contrapositive of q, then q is equivalent to the contrapositive of r. For instance, if q is "All S are P," then r, its contrapositive, is "All nonP are nonS." But what is the contrapositive of r? If we transpose the subject and predicate of r and negate each of them, we obtain "All non-nonS are non-nonP"; letting the double negations within the terms cancel out, we have "All S are P," which is exactly q.

The relation between an A sentence and its converse by limitation is not a symmetrical relation, however. Instead, it is asymmetrical. If r is the converse by limitation of q, then q never is the converse by limitation of r.

EXERCISE 6

*A In each case state how the conclusion is related to the premise (converse, obverse, etc.); and say whether the argument is valid, indicating whether any existential presupposition makes a difference.

   1 All Kenyans are Africans. Hence, no Kenyans are non-Africans.
   2 No sibyls are prophets. Therefore, no prophets are sibyls.
   3 Some submarines are warships. So some submarines are not nonwarships.
   4 All tomatoes are vegetables. So all vegetables are tomatoes.
   5 Some sailing ships are merchant ships. So some merchant ships are sailing ships.
   6 All oranges are fruits. So all nonfruits are nonoranges.
   7 Some plays are not comedies. So some plays are noncomedies.

8 Some stars are not luminous bodies. So some luminous bodies are not stars.

9 Some judges are septuagenarians. So some nonseptuagenarians are nonjudges.

10 No passenger vessels are submarines. So all passenger vessels are nonsubmarines.

11 Some logicians are not mathematicians. So some nonmathematicians are not nonlogicians.

12 All scarabs are beetles. So some beetles are scarabs.

13 No spiders are insects. So no noninsects are nonspiders.

14 Some Yugoslavs are non-Christians. So some Yugoslavs are not Christians.

15 All Senegalese are non-Asians. So no Senegalese are Asians.

16 All chairs are not nonthrones. So some chairs are thrones.

17 No supermarkets are nonstores. So all supermarkets are stores.

18 All secretaries are executives. So all executives are secretaries.

19 No nonsandwiches are nonpizzas. So no pizzas are sandwiches.

20 All nonmammals are nonwalruses. So all walruses are mammals.

B By what sequence of steps can the second sentence be validly inferred from the first? Operations of immediate inference and relationships from the square of opposition may be used. Make clear any existential presuppositions.

1 No Africans are Buddhists. Some Africans are non-Buddhists.

2 Some metals are liquids. Some liquids are not nonmetals.

3 No Greek epics are poems about courtly love. Some poems about courtly love are not Greek epics.

4 No Senators are adolescents. All adolescents are non-Senators.

5 All Burmese are Asians. Some Asians are not non-Burmese.

6 All insects are nonquadrupeds. All quadrupeds are noninsects.

7 No sharks are cetaceans. Some nonsharks are cetaceans.

8 All spies are criminals. Some nonspies are noncriminals.

9 Some songs are not anthems. Some nonanthems are songs.

10 All astrologers are nonscientists. Some nonscientists are not nonastrologers.

C Explain why each argument is not valid.

1 No Mongolians are vegetarians. So no Mongolians are nonvegetarians.

2 All rabbis are religious leaders. So all religious leaders are rabbis.

3 All bureaucrats are officials. So all officials are bureaucrats.

4 Some luxury cars are not sportscars. So some sportscars are not luxury cars.

5 No nonresidents are members of the council. So all residents are members of the council.

6 Some sons of his are not fat giants. So some sons of his are nonfat giants.

7 Some volcanic eruptions are catastrophes. So some noncatastrophes are not volcanic eruptions.

8 All French generals are dignified patriots. So all undignified patriots are non-French generals.

9 Some numbers are not rational. So some numbers are not nonrational.

10 No members of the faculty are unrecognized geniuses. So all members of the faculty are recognized geniuses.

7 THE SYLLOGISM

An argument is a *categorical syllogism* (or *syllogism*, for short) just in case it consists of three categorical sentences containing three terms in all, each term appearing in two different sentences. The argument "All Pakistanis are Moslems; no Sinhalese are Moslems; therefore no Sinhalese are Pakistanis" is an example of a syllogism. It consists of three categorical sentences that contain three different terms, each term appearing in two different sentences.

The term appearing as the predicate of the conclusion (in this case "Pakistanis") is called the *major term* of the syllogism. The term appearing as the subject of the conclusion (in this case "Sinhalese") is called the *minor term* of the syllogism. And the term appearing in the premises but not in the conclusion is called the *middle term*. The premise containing the major term is called the *major premise*, and the premise containing the minor term is called the *minor premise*. For the sake of having a standard procedure, let us follow the traditional convention and always put the major premise first, then the minor premise, and last the conclusion.

The example just given is a syllogism whose logical form is:

All P are M
No S are M
$\therefore$ no S are P

To give the *mood* of a syllogism is to state the categorical forms of its sentences. We mention these in the standard order: major premise, minor premise, conclusion. In our example of a syllogism, its major premise is an **A** sentence, its minor premise is an **E** and its conclusion is an **E**. Therefore, this particular syllogism is in the mood **AEE**.

But there is more to say about its form, for other different syllogisms can share with it this mood **AEE**. For instance, a syllogism also is in the mood **AEE** if it has the structure:

All M are P
No S are M
$\therefore$ no S are P

This sort of syllogism differs from the previous kind because of the different arrangement of its terms; and the difference is important, for one syllogism is valid, the other invalid. Saying how its terms are arranged within the sentences in which they occur is called giving the *figure* of the syllogism.

There are four different figures that syllogisms have, that is, four different ways in which the terms can be arranged. We can represent these four figures as follows:

1		2		3		4	
M	P	P	M	M	P	P	M
S	M	S	M	M	S	M	S
S	P	S	P	S	P	S	P

Here "S" is the minor term, "P" is the major term, and "M" is the middle term. It is easy to remember which figure is which if we think of the positions of the middle term as outlining the front of a shirt collar (Figure 18). The first form of syllogism we considered was **AEE** in the second figure; the second form was **AEE** in the first figure.

Any two syllogisms having the same mood and figure always are alike as regards whether their form is valid. If one is valid in form, the other will be too—because mood and figure are the only features that count. Then how many different forms of syllogisms are possible? There are four possibilities regarding the form of the major premise (**A, E, I, O**), four possibilities regarding the form of the minor premise, four possibilities regarding the form of the conclusion, and four possibilities regarding the figure of the syllogism. This means that there are 4 × 4 × 4 × 4, or 256, possible forms in all. A large majority of these forms are invalid, however.

How can we tell whether a given form of syllogism is valid? Venn diagrams provide the most straightforward method. The method is this: We draw a diagram showing exactly what the two premises of the syllogism say; then, by looking at it, we can see whether or not the conclusion necessarily follows from those premises. It can follow only if it is already contained in the premises.

The syllogism "All Pakistanis are Moslems; no Sinhalese are Moslems; therefore no Sinhalese are Pakistanis" is in the mood **AEE** and in the second figure, as we saw. Let us adopt the hypothetical viewpoint as we investigate the validity of this syllogism (actually, it makes no real difference in this case; later we shall consider how to bring in an existential viewpoint). To test the validity of this syllogism, we form a diagram showing exactly what the premises say. Since the premises contain three terms, the diagram must

Figure 18

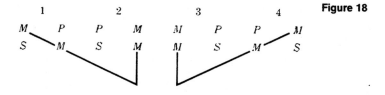

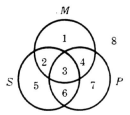

Figure 19

show relations among three classes of beings: Pakistanis, Sinhalese, and Moslems (Figure 19).

We now imagine that all Moslems are herded inside the M circle, they alone being allowed in it. All Pakistanis are put inside the P circle, nothing but Pakistanis being allowed there. And all Sinhalese are confined to the S circle, which non-Sinhalese may not enter. We must be sure to begin the diagram by drawing three circles that overlap in such a way as to allow for all possible subclasses formed by these three given classes. The circles must overlap so as to yield eight distinct regions on the diagram, for there are eight distinct subclasses which we must be able to consider.

Region 1 of the diagram is the location of Moslems who are not Sinhalese and not Pakistanis. Region 2 would contain Moslems who are Sinhalese but who are not Pakistanis. In region 3 would be found Moslems who are Sinhalese and also Pakistanis. Region 4 would contain Moslems who are Pakistanis but not Sinhalese. Region 5 is the location of Sinhalese who are neither Moslems nor Pakistanis. Region 6 is for Sinhalese who are Pakistanis but not Moslems. Region 7 is the place for Pakistanis who are neither Sinhalese nor Moslems. And region 8 is occupied by those who are neither Moslems nor Sinhalese nor Pakistanis.

The major premise of our syllogism declares that all Pakistanis are Moslems. This means that all who are inside the P circle are inside the M circle; that is, that the part of the P circle outside the M circle is unoccupied. We indicate this on the diagram by crossing out regions 6 and 7 (Figure 20). The minor premise of the syllogism declares that no Sinhalese are Moslems. This means that all who are inside the S circle are outside the M circle; that is, that part of the S circle which is inside the M circle is unoccupied. We indicate this by crossing out regions 2 and 3 (Figure 21). We now have a diagram that shows exactly what the premises say, no more and no less.

We now inspect the diagram to see whether or not the argument is valid. According to the diagram, all that part of the S circle which overlaps the P circle is unoccupied. That is, there are no Sinhalese who are Pakistanis. This means that the conclusion validly follows from the premises; if the premises are true, the conclusion must necessarily be true also.

If you have difficulty telling whether the diagram shows the argument to

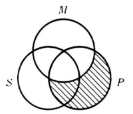

Figure 20

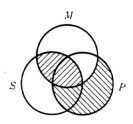

Figure 21

be valid, try this: See whether it is logically possible to add the *contradictory* of the conclusion to the diagram for the premises. If this is possible, the argument is invalid. If it is impossible, the argument is valid. In the syllogism which we have just been considering, the contradictory of the conclusion would be "Some Sinhalese are Pakistanis"; to add this to the diagram of Figure 21 would be impossible, for it would mean putting an asterisk into an area that is entirely crossed out. This helps us to see how the diagram shows the argument to be valid.

Next let us consider the syllogism "All Mormons are pious persons; no Samoans are Mormons; therefore no Samoans are pious persons." This syllogism is in the mood **AEE** and in the first figure. To test its validity, we again draw a diagram that will show exactly what the premises say. The major premise tells us that whatever is inside the M circle is inside the P circle; that is, that the part of the M circle outside the P circle is unoccupied. Accordingly we cross out regions 1 and 2 (Figure 22). The minor premise tells us that nothing inside the S circle is inside the M circle; that is, that the part of the S circle overlapping the M circle is unoccupied. So we add to our diagram by crossing out regions 2 and 3 (Figure 23). Here the completed diagram shows that the syllogism is invalid. For according to the diagram it may or may not be that Samoans are pious persons.

In dealing with the syllogism "All warriors are heroes; some Greeks are not warriors; therefore some Greeks are not heroes," special care must be taken in drawing the diagram. To indicate the major premise is easy (Figure

Figure 22

Figure 23

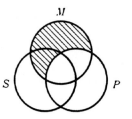

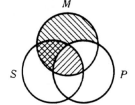

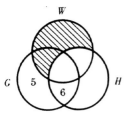

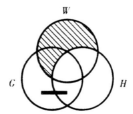

Figure 24   Figure 25

24). But the minor premise gives trouble, for we wish to indicate on the diagram exactly the information expressed, no less and no more. The minor premise is a particular sentence, and it declares that a certain space on the diagram is occupied. But what space? To put an asterisk in region 5 would be to claim that the premise tells us there are Greeks who are neither warriors nor heroes; this is more than what the premise says. To put an asterisk in region 6 would be to claim that the premise tells us there are Greeks who are heroes but not warriors; this too is more than the premise says. All the premise says is that there is at least one individual either in region 5 or in region 6 (although there may be individuals in both places).

The best way to draw the diagram is to use a bar instead of an asterisk. We draw a bar touching region 5 and region 6 but no other regions (Figure 25); we interpret this to mean that there is something somewhere in the space the bar touches. Thus, according to the diagram, there may or may not be Greeks who are not heroes; when the premises are true, the conclusion of the syllogism may or may not be true. We see by the diagram that this **AOO** first-figure syllogism is invalid.

Using the same method, we can deal with the syllogism "No astronauts are Buddhists; some vegetarians are Buddhists; therefore some vegetarians are not astronauts." This syllogism is in the mood **EIO** and in the second figure. When we draw our diagram (Figure 26), we find that the diagram shows the syllogism to be valid. In handling a syllogism like this with one universal and one particular premise, it is good strategy first to enter on the

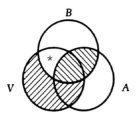

Figure 26

diagram what the universal premise says. Then it may be easier to enter what the particular premise says. If we had entered the particular premise on the diagram first, we would have had to use a bar; then, in entering the universal premise, we would have crossed out half the bar—in effect turning it into an asterisk.

Various generalizations can be made concerning how the diagrams for valid syllogisms must look. For instance, any syllogism whose Venn diagram contains exactly three shaded regions is invalid. And any syllogism is invalid whose Venn diagram contains a bar that touches more than one region (that is, if the syllogism is to be valid, the bar must have been shaded out of all but one region). However, it is better to understand how to use Venn diagrams than to memorize mechanical rules like these.

Now we must consider how an existential viewpoint can make a difference to the validity of a syllogism. With many syllogisms, such as those we have just been considering, presuppositions about existence make no difference to whether the syllogisms are valid. However, there are a few cases where this does make a difference. All these are syllogisms having two universal premises and a particular conclusion. For instance, consider the syllogism "No minors medically fit for military service are paraplegics; all students who can run a mile in four minutes are minors medically fit for military service; therefore, some students who can run a mile in four minutes are not paraplegics."

Figure 27 shows how we can diagram what the premises say. In drawing the left-hand diagram, we adopt the hypothetical viewpoint and leave it an open question as to whether individuals of any of these types exist; from this viewpoint, the syllogism is invalid. However, if we may assume the existence of students who can run a mile in four minutes, then we may add an asterisk to the diagram, and now the conclusion will follow (see the right-hand diagram). Thus this form of syllogism is invalid from the hypothetical viewpoint, but is valid from a certain existential viewpoint (notice that for this particular form of syllogism it happens to be an assumption about S's, not about M's or P's, that is required).

In this case there does not seem to be any obvious reason for regarding

Figure 27

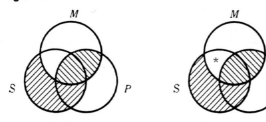

one viewpoint as more appropriate than the other. Perhaps in the context of an actual discussion it would be clear which viewpoint should be adopted; but when we are discussing the syllogism abstractly, the best we can do is to explain the situation, pointing out the ambiguity, and leave matters at that.

EXERCISE 7

*A For each syllogism, determine its mood and figure, and test its validity by means of a Venn diagram.

1 All ruminants are mammals. All cattle are ruminants. Therefore, all cattle are mammals.
2 No pharmacists are lawyers. Some realtors are lawyers. So some realtors are not pharmacists.
3 All existentialists are metaphysicians. Some pragmatists are not existentialists. So some pragmatists are not metaphysicians.
4 No predators are ruminants. All sheep are ruminants. So no sheep are predators.
5 No figs are coconuts. No dates are coconuts. So no dates are figs.
6 No galleys are caravels. Some merchant ships are galleys. So some merchant ships are not caravels.
7 No Basques are Normans. Some Flemings are not Normans. So some Flemings are not Basques.
8 All anarchists are radicals. No conservatives are radicals. So no conservatives are anarchists.
9 Some nations are monarchies. Some language communities are not nations. So some language communities are not monarchies.
10 Some marsupials are carnivores. All carnivores are predators. So some predators are marsupials.
11 All Bavarians are Germans. No Bavarians are Rhinelanders. So no Rhinelanders are Germans.
12 All shot-putters are athletes. Some shot-putters are overweight persons. So some overweight persons are athletes.
13 All Hegelians are idealists. Some idealists are not theists. So some theists are not Hegelians.
14 All geometers are mathematicians. Some logicians are not mathematicians. So some logicians are not geometers.
15 No motorcycles are limousines. All motorcycles are fast vehicles. So no fast vehicles are limousines.

B Determine the mood and figure of each of the following syllogisms, test it by a Venn diagram, and discuss whether it should be classified as valid.

1 No persons who can run a 3-minute mile are Americans. All persons who can run a 3-minute mile are great athletes. So some great athletes are not Americans.
2 All natives of Tokyo are Japanese. No Japanese are blondes. So some blondes are not natives of Tokyo.
3 All contest winners are residents of this city. No Martians are residents of this city. So some Martians are not contest winners.

4 No inexpensive articles are good buys. Some mink-lined sneakers are not inexpensive articles. So some mink-lined sneakers are good buys.

5 All vagrants are homeless persons. All homeless persons are needy persons. So some needy persons are vagrants.

6 All friends of mine are people on the team. Some friends of mine are people 7 feet tall. So some people 7 feet tall are people on the team.

7 All persons whom we want on the team are students who play well. No students who play well are persons 9 feet tall. So some persons 9 feet tall are not persons whom we want on the team.

8 All even numbers are whole numbers. No transcendental numbers are whole numbers. So some transcendental numbers are not even numbers.

8 RULES OF THE SYLLOGISM

Venn diagrams provide an efficient and general method for determining the validity of any syllogism. If we were to construct a Venn diagram for each of the 64 possible kinds of premises that the 256 possible forms of syllogism can have (32 diagrams would do; a tedious but instructive exercise), we would find that the following 15 forms are the only ones valid from the hypothetical viewpoint:

Figure 1	Figure 2	Figure 3	Figure 4
AAA	EAE	IAI	AEE
EAE	AEE	AII	IAI
AII	EIO	OAO	EIO
EIO	AOO	EIO	

Nine additional forms are valid, provided that appropriate existential presuppositions are made[12]:

Figure 1	Figure 2	Figure 3	Figure 4	Presupposition required
AAI EAO	AEO EAO		AEO	S exist
		AAI EAO	EAO	M exist
			AAI	P exist

It is not necessary to memorize this list of valid forms. It is far better to remember how to test syllogisms for validity. Venn diagrams provide one method for testing them. But on the basis of this list, we can develop another method which does not require paper and pencil. If we study this list of valid forms of syllogisms, we can verify certain rules that valid syllogisms obey. One set of rules is the following:

1 In any valid syllogism the middle term is distributed at least once.

2 In any valid syllogism every term distributed in the conclusion is distributed in a premise (but note that this rule allows a term to be distributed in a premise without being distributed in the conclusion).

3 No valid syllogism has two negative premises.

4 Any valid syllogism has at least one negative premise if and only if it has a negative conclusion.

5 No syllogism valid from the hypothetical viewpoint has two universal premises and a particular conclusion.

If we studied the list of valid forms (which we can justify by appeal to Venn diagrams), we could prove that each of these rules is correct.

What do we mean by calling one thing a necessary condition, or a sufficient condition, for another? By saying that *B* is a *necessary* condition for *C*, we mean that nothing is a case of *C* without being a case of *B*. For example, being at least thirty years old is a necessary condition for being a United States senator. By saying that *B* is a *sufficient* condition for *C*, we mean that anything which is a case of *B* is a case of *C*. For example, eating a pint of arsenic is a sufficient condition for promptly dying.

Given that we know by Venn diagrams which forms of syllogisms are valid and which are invalid, we can establish some noteworthy facts about the above set of rules. Each of the first four rules states a necessary condition for the validity of a syllogism regarded from an existential viewpoint. Furthermore, taken together, the requirements stated in these first four rules constitute a sufficient condition for the validity of a syllogism regarded from an existential viewpoint. Also, each of the five rules states a necessary condition for the validity of a syllogism regarded from the hypothetical viewpoint. And taken together, all five rules constitute a sufficient condition for the validity of such a syllogism.

Once we have established these rules, we may use them instead of Venn diagrams for checking the validity of syllogisms. To use the rules in testing the validity of a particular syllogism, we simply observe whether the syllogism breaks any one of the rules; if it breaks a rule, it is invalid, and if it breaks no rule, it is valid.

A syllogism that breaks the first rule is said to commit the fallacy of *undistributed middle*. A syllogism that breaks the second rule is said to commit a fallacy of *illicit process*; it is *illicit process of the major* if the major term is distributed in the conclusion but not in the major premise, and it is *illicit process of the minor* if the minor term is distributed in the conclusion but not in the minor premise. No special names are given to violations of the other rules.

Old-fashioned logic books usually also give the rule "A syllogism must have only three terms." Violation of this rule was called the *fallacy of four terms*. But it is unnecessary for us to include this rule in our list since by definition a syllogism must have just three terms. The fallacy of four terms is a special kind of equivocation (which will be discussed in Chapter 6).

The set of rules stated above has been chosen so as to constitute a brief and easily remembered criterion for the validity of any syllogism. It is also of interest to see how additional rules can be deduced from this initial set of rules. For example, if we wish to prove that no valid syllogism has two particular premises (i.e., that every valid syllogism has at least one universal premise), we can reason as follows:

Suppose that there was a valid syllogism having two particular premises. Its premises would be either (1) two **I** sentences, or (2) two **O** sentences, or (3) and **I** and an **O**. Case 1 is excluded by rule 1, since in two **I** premises the middle term would nowhere be distributed. Case 2 is excluded by rule 3. Case 3 would require the conclusion to be negative, according to rule 4; and in a negative sentence the predicate is distributed, so that by rule 2 the major term would have to be distributed in the major premise. But by rule 1 the middle term would also have to be distributed somewhere in a premise. However, it is impossible for both the major and the middle term to be distributed, since an **I** and an **O** premise contain only one distributed term altogether. Therefore case 3 is excluded, for it would commit either the fallacy of undistributed middle or the fallacy of illicit process of the major. Hence, the rules imply that there can be no valid syllogism having two particular premises.

EXERCISE 8

   *A Go back to part A of Exercise 7, and test each of those syllogisms by means of the rules of the syllogism.

   B Identify the mood and figure of each of the following syllogisms. Test its validity by means of the rules. Then check your answer with a Venn diagram, and name any fallacy that has a name.

     1 No Methodists are Lutherans. Some Danes are Lutherans. So some Danes are not Methodists.

     2 Some epic poems are not sagas. No epic poems are comedies. So some comedies are sagas.

     3 No koalas are bears. All grizzlies are bears. So some grizzlies are not koalas.

     4 No philologists are semanticists. Some classicists are philologists. So some classicists are semanticists.

     5 No primates are marsupials. All lemurs are primates. So no lemurs are marsupials.

     6 All hexagons are rectilinear figures. All pentagons are rectilinear figures. So all pentagons are hexagons.

     7 All battleships are warships. No warships are sailing ships. So some sailing ships are not battleships.

     8 All tracts are essays. Some poems are essays. So some poems are tracts.

     9 All detectives are sleuths. Some policemen are detectives. So some policemen are sleuths.

    10 All atheists are positivists, since all positivists are materialists, and all materialists are atheists.

11 All poachers are intruders. Hence, all poachers are trespassers, for some intruders are trespassers.

12 Some seats of government are not metropolises, because some metropolises are not capitals, and all seats of government are capitals.

C Appealing only to the first four rules of the syllogism, prove that the following generalizations hold for all syllogisms valid from an existential viewpoint.

1 If one premise is particular, the conclusion is particular.

2 In the first figure the minor premise is affirmative.

3 In the first figure the major premise is universal.

4 In the second figure the conclusion is negative.

5 In the second figure the major premise is universal.

6 In the third figure the conclusion is particular.

7 In the third figure the minor premise is affirmative.

8 If the major term is the predicate of the major premise, then the minor premise is affirmative.

9 In the fourth figure, if the conclusion is negative, the major premise is universal.

10 In the fourth figure, if the minor premise is affirmative, the conclusion is particular.

†D Appealing to the syllogistic rules, prove your answers to the following questions. For all but the first question, adopt an existential viewpoint.

1 Can a syllogism be valid from the hypothetical viewpoint but not from an existential viewpoint?

2 In what syllogisms, if any, is the middle term distributed in both premises?

3 Can an invalid syllogism violate all four rules at once?

4 What is the maximum number of rules that an invalid syllogism can violate at once?

5 How many more occurrences of distributed terms can there be in the premises of a valid syllogism than there are in its conclusion?

6 In what valid syllogism is the major term distributed in the major premise but not in the conclusion? Prove that there is just one such syllogism.

9 TRANSLATING INTO STANDARD FORM

So far, we have been considering arguments that are in standard form. Our rules for the syllogism, for instance, are supposed to apply only to arguments that are strictly in standard syllogistic form. But few of the arguments we meet in ordinary discourse are exactly in standard form. To make our logical rules more widely useful, we need to understand that many arguments which are not quite in standard form can be put into standard form so as to be testable by our rules.

Putting Sentences into Categorical Form

Arguments in ordinary discourse often contain sentences which are not categorical—this is one way in which ordinary arguments can fail to have the standard form that we want. However, any sentence can be translated into an equivalent standard-form categorical sentence, if we exercise ingenuity (indeed, there are always various acceptable ways of doing this, if we do not mind awkwardness, and if all we are looking for is a standard-form sentence equivalent to the original).[13] Let us think about some examples of such translations.

When a sentence fails to be categorical merely because its predicate is an adjective, we can supply a noun. Thus, "All tigers are carnivorous" can become "All tigers are carnivorous animals," and "No realtors are altruistic" can become "No realtors are altruists."

Where a sentence contains a verb other than "are," we can convert the sentence into standard form by moving the old verb into the predicate. Thus, "All cats eat mice" can become "All cats are animals that eat mice" or "All cats are mouse-eaters." "Some Senators seek reelection" can become "Some Senators are seekers of reelection."

Sentences containing the verb "to be" in the past tense or future tense can be put into categorical form by moving the tensed verb into the predicate. Thus "Some Elizabethans are people who were lovers of bear baiting" can replace "Some Elizabethans were people who loved bear baiting." Similarly, "No rich men will enter into the Kingdom of Heaven" can become "No rich men are people who will enter the Kingdom of Heaven." These examples illustrate how, in a categorical sentence, the copula is to be understood in a tenseless sense.

Sentences in which the word order is different from our standard form can be realigned. Thus "Jaguars are all fast cars" can become "All Jaguar cars are fast cars." (Notice that it would be misleading to use the translation "All Jaguar cars are fast things," for here the word "fast" has a meaning that is comparative—Jaguars are fast for cars, though they are not fast compared with jet planes.) As another example, "No lazy workers are the bees" can become "No bees are lazy workers."

Some further examples: "Elephants never are carnivorous" can become "No elephants are carnivorous creatures." And "There are abstemious sailors" can become "Some sailors are abstemious persons." In each case we try to construct in categorical form a new sentence that is equivalent to the original one.

Sentences like "Ohio is a state" and "Caesar conquered Gaul" seem to pose a problem. We cannot translate the former into "All Ohio is a state," because this has the wrong copula and because its subject term is not a general term (it is a proper name instead—a kind of singular term). To translate it into "All parts of Ohio are states" would be wrong because this is not equivalent to the original. The best way is to translate it into "All things identical to Ohio are states." This translation sounds artificial, but it provides a sentence in proper categorical form that necessarily agrees with the original sentence as regards truth and falsity, since one and only one thing is identical to Ohio (that is, Ohio itself). Similarly, "Caesar conquered Gaul" can become "All persons identical to Caesar are people who were conquerors of Gaul." This somewhat cumbersome style of translation is appropriate only for handling singular terms, however; it would be pointless to translate "All Jaguars are fast cars" into "All things identical to Jaguars are fast cars."

Sometimes we meet sentences that contain no specific indication of quantity. Occasionally such sentences are really ambiguous, but often if we think about how they would be used, we can see that they mean one thing rather than the other. Thus, someone who says "Bachelors are unmarried" surely intends to say "*All* bachelors are unmarried persons," while someone who says "Visitors are coming" surely intends to say "*Some* visitors are coming." Similarly, "An elephant is a pachyderm" surely is equivalent to "All elephants are pachyderms," but "A police officer is at the door" is equivalent to "Some police officers are persons at the door."

Another sort of ambiguity can occur when the word "not" is inserted in the middle of a universal sentence. Does it belong to the copula or to the predicate? "All my professors are not boring" might be equivalent to "All professors of mine are people who are not boring," or it might be equivalent to "It is not the case that all professors of mine are people who are boring," that is, "Some professors of mine are not people who are boring." When we meet a sentence constructed in this ambiguous way, we have to try to guess what the speaker means.

Sentences containing the words "only" and "none but" must be handled carefully. "Only Midwesterners attend Calvin Coolidge College" does not mean that all Midwesterners are attenders of C.C.C.; what it means is "All persons who attend C.C.C. are midwesterners." Similarly, "None but the brave deserve the fair" does not mean that all brave persons are deservers of the fair; it means "All persons who deserve the fair are brave persons." In general, "Only S are P" and "None but S are P" both are equivalent to "All P are S."

However, "only some" has a meaning different from "only" by itself. Thus "Only some pigs eat acorns" means "Some pigs are eaters of acorns and some pigs are not eaters of acorns." In a similar vein, "All except employees are eligible" means "All nonemployees are eligible," and it strongly *suggests*, although it does not necessarily *say*, that no employees are eligible—whether it should ever be interpreted as implying that no employees are eligible is arguable. Similarly, "Anyone is eligible unless he is an employee" means "All nonemployees are eligible," and it too suggests, though it does not necessarily say, that no employees are eligible. In general, both "All except S are P" and "Anything is P unless it is S" imply "All nonS are P," and it is ambiguous whether they also imply "No S are P."

Sometimes we may have to devise entirely new terms before we can put a sentence into categorical form. The sentence "Whenever it rains, it pours" does not look like a categorical sentence, but if we think of it as a remark about *times*, we can see that it is equivalent to "All times when it rains are times when it pours." Similarly, "Wherever you go, I will go" can be understood as referring to places, and it can become "All places where you go are places where I will go." However, we have to be alert to the intended meanings of sentences like these. "Wilbur always sleeps in class" probably does not mean "All times are times when Wilbur sleeps in class"; surely the intended meaning is more likely to be "All times when Wilbur is in class are times during which he does some sleeping." Similarly, "She goes everywhere with him" probably does not mean "All places are places to which she goes with him"; much more likely it means "All places he goes are places where she goes with him."

Working out translations such as these will often be necessary as a preliminary to the syllogistic analysis of ordinary reasoning. But it also has an additional intellectual value in that it encourages us to understand more accurately what ordinary sentences are saying.

Translating into Syllogistic Form

Many arguments that are not in syllogistic form as they stand can nevertheless be translated legitimately into syllogisms. That is, their premises and conclusions admit of being translated into equivalent categorical sentences that do form syllogisms, and the validity of the original arguments stands or falls with that of the standard syllogisms into which they are translated. By translating arguments in this way, we make it easier to test their validity by means of Venn diagrams, and we make it possible to test their validity by the rules of the syllogism.

There are two different respects in which an argument that can be translated into a syllogism may at first fall short of being in standard syllogistic form. The argument may at first contain sentences that are not categorical, or it may at first contain more than three terms. How shall we deal with syllogistic arguments that contain too many terms?

Suppose we have an argument that looks like a syllogism, in that it contains three sentences and talks about just three classes of things. However, it contains too many terms, some of these terms being negations (contradictories) of others. When this happens, we can use operations such as obversion or contraposition to eliminate some of the terms, replacing some original sentences by equivalent new ones. For instance, consider the argument "No millionaires are paupers; no stars of television are non-millionaires; therefore no stars of television are paupers." The argument is not in syllogistic form as it stands, because it contains four terms. But two of its terms are contradictories, and so if we obvert the second premise, we can change the argument into the form "No M are P. All S are M. So no S are P." Now it is a standard syllogism (**EAE** in the first figure, and valid).

Notice that it would have been an error to have called the original argument invalid because it contained two negative premises. The rule that an argument with two negative premises is invalid applies only to syllogisms in standard form (and the same goes for all our syllogistic rules). We should not try to apply the rules until after we have got the argument into standard form.

When some terms are contradictories of others, obversion and contraposition can often allow us to reword an argument so as to reduce the number of terms. But sometimes a deeper rewording of an argument is required if we are to put it into syllogistic form. Where this is so, we must be thoughtful about selecting our terms, trying to word the argument so that we have just three terms in all, each of which appears in two different sentences of the argument. For instance, consider the argument "The car doesn't start easily when the temperature is below zero; it will be below zero tomorrow; so tomorrow the car won't start easily." Although this does not look much like a syllogism, we can get it into syllogistic form. One way is this: "All days when the temperature falls below zero are days when the car does not start easily; all days identical to tomorrow are days when the temperature falls below zero; therefore, all days identical to tomorrow are days when the car does not start easily." Here we have **AAA** in the first figure, and it is valid.

EXERCISE 9

   *A Translate each sentence into an equivalent sentence in categorical form, trying to interpret it in the way most likely to be intended.

    1 All ducks are aquatic.
    2 Some concerts are not boring.
    3 A Rolls Royce is very costly.
    4 Tadpoles never become snakes.
    5 There are fortress monasteries.
    6 There are no unclimbed mountains.
    7 All cashiers are not courteous.
    8 Whoever spies for a foreign power commits treason.
    9 Only Esquimos live in Greenland.
   10 The dinosaurs were made extinct by a change of climate.
   11 A fish has scales.
   12 Ithaca was the home of Odysseus.
   13 Whatever you buy in Paris will be stylish.
   14 Nothing but aspirin helps my headache.
   15 Wherever there are oaks, acorns will be found.
   16 All violators will be prosecuted.
   17 Whenever he felt homesick he would get drunk.
   18 My car always starts with difficulty.
   19 The llama is wooly.
   20 The Minotaur was slain by Theseus.

   *B Put each argument into syllogistic form, explaining your steps. Name the resulting mood and figure, and test its validity by a Venn diagram and by the rules.

1 A noncitizen is a nonvoter. No resident alien is a citizen. So some resident aliens are not voters.

2 It's not the case that some Brazilians are not South Americans. Uzbeks never are South Americans. So no Uzbeks are Brazilians.

3 No sharks aren't fish. So a hammerhead is a fish, since a hammerhead is a shark.

4 Straight lines never curve. Only straight lines are the sides of triangles. So the sides of triangles never curve.

5 Nothing but ghosts are poltergeists. Hence, no succubus is a ghost, since a succubus never is a poltergeist.

6 There aren't any carthorses that are racehorses. Hence, old Dobbin isn't a racehorse, for he's a carthorse.

7 Africans never are Hindus, since only non-Hindus are Egyptians, and Egyptians always are Africans.

8 Some dictatorships are not nonmonarchies. In a monarchy a king is the head of state. So some states headed by kings are not dictatorships.

9 Some nonoceans are not nonseas. All lakes are nonoceans. So lakes sometimes aren't seas.

10 Whoever isn't a friend of Mil's isn't a friend of Phil's. So, friends of Sal's never are friends of Phil's, since there are no friends of Mil's who are friends of Sal's.

11 There are mice that aren't prolific. No mice are nonrodents. So rodents sometimes are nonprolific.

12 Grandmothers never go in for surfing. Surfers sometimes go in for sunbathing. So no sunbathers are grandmothers.

13 Wherever the soil is very acid, flowers won't grow. But flowers grow in your garden, so the soil can't be very acid there.

14 You can't convict someone of murder just on circumstantial evidence. There is only circumstantial evidence against the butler. So the butler can't be convicted of murder.

15 Anytime the press is free there will be active criticism of the government. You never get active criticism of the government without some of it being unfair. So you can't have a free press without some unfair criticism of the government.

C Translate each sentence into categorical form, trying to interpret as it is likely to be intended.

1 Blessed are the peacemakers.
2 None but the lonely heart can know my sadness.
3 He jests at scars who never felt a wound.
4 Who lives without folly is not so wise as he thinks.
5 Tardiness is reprehensible.
6 There never was a philosopher that could endure the toothache patiently.
7 He cannot become rich who will not labor.
8 No news is good news.
9 No friend is better than a fair-weather friend.
10 Whoever loves me loves my dog.
11 Those who live in glass houses shouldn't throw stones.
12 It is a wise father that knows his own child.

13 None but those who love virtue love angling.
14 Except ye be as little children, ye shall not enter into the kingdom of God.
15 It is sharper than a serpent's tooth to have an ungrateful child.

10 RELATED TYPES OF ARGUMENT

We can make use of what we now know about syllogisms and about Venn diagrams in order to analyze some additional arguments that are a little different from the types we have studied so far.

The Sorites

Sometimes we encounter an argument that can be interpreted as a chain, or sequence, of syllogisms. This means that two premises of the original argument can be combined to form a syllogism, whose conclusion can then be combined with another premise from the original argument to form another, whose conclusion can then be combined with another premise from the original argument to form yet another syllogism, and so on, until we reach the final conclusion. An argument of this type is called a *sorites* (from the Greek word for a pile).

In order to show that a sorites is valid, we must show how it is possible to pass, by a series of valid syllogistic steps, from the premises to the conclusion. We use our ingenuity in order to fit together the links of the chain, testing each link by means of a Venn diagram or by the rules of the syllogism.

For example, consider the argument:

Some prime numbers are integers.	(1)
All rational numbers are real numbers.	(2)
All integers are rational numbers	(3)
Therefore, some prime numbers are real numbers.	(4)

This may be symbolized:

Some P are I.	(1)
All Ra are Re.	(2)
All I are Ra.	(3)
$\therefore$ some P are Re.	(4)

Here (1) and (3) can be combined to make a syllogism of the form **AII** in the first figure; their conclusion, "Some P are Ra," can then be combined with (2) to make a syllogism again of the form **AII** in the first figure; its conclusion is (4). Thus we show that the original premises validly yield the desired result.

The method just employed is a method for establishing the validity of a valid sorites. Suppose, however, that in a given case we try to pass, by means of syllogistic steps, from the premises to the conclusion but do not find a way to do so. This may lead us to *suspect* that the sorites is invalid, but just by itself our failure does not definitely *prove* that the sorites is invalid. Perhaps we simply have not been ingenious enough. To prove that the sorites is invalid by using our present method, we would have to investigate *every* possible sequence in which the premises might have been combined, and we would have to show that *none* of these sequences validly yields the conclusion.

Further Uses of Venn Diagrams

Some arguments that cannot be translated into syllogisms or into chains of syllogisms can nevertheless be tested by means of Venn diagrams. Consider the argument "Every student of theology studies Greek or studies Hebrew. Some students of theology do not study Hebrew. So not all who study Greek study Hebrew." We may rewrite this argument in the form:

> All *T* are (*G* or *H*).
> Some *T* are not *H*.
> ∴ some *G* are not *H*.

Here we have an argument that is not valid as a syllogism, for if we think of it as containing just three terms, then its premises are not all in categorical form; while if we think of its premises as in categorical form, then there are more than three terms ("*T*," "*H*," "*G*," and "*G* or *H*").

But we would be too hasty if we assumed this argument to be invalid just because it is not a valid syllogism. This kind of argument is not supposed to be a syllogism. It is a kind of argument, however, whose validity can be tested by means of a Venn diagram, since it deals with just three classes of individuals and makes appropriately simple assertions about them. We can test it by making a diagram which shows exactly what the premises say; then we can inspect the diagram to see whether the conclusion follows.

Here our diagram needs three circles, representing those who study theology, those who study Greek, and those who study Hebrew. The first premise declares that all individuals inside the *T* circle are either inside the *G* circle or inside the *H* circle (we interpret the premise as not intending to exclude the possibility that some who are in *T* may be in *G* and *H* both). This means that none who are inside the *T* circle are outside both the *G* and *H* circles (Figure 28). The second premise makes the added claim that some individuals inside the *T* circle are outside the *H* circle (Figure 29). Inspecting the completed diagram, we see that the conclusion that not all who are inside the *G* circle are inside the *H* circle validly follows.

EXERCISE 10

*A Use appropriate methods to deal with these arguments.
  1 Whatever Allie likes, Bud likes. Allie likes nothing that Cal likes. Everything Dan likes, Cal likes. So Bud likes nothing Dan likes.

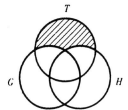

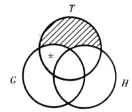

Figure 28   Figure 29

2 No one European is Chinese. Everyone Scandinavian is European. Everyone Swedish is Scandinavian. Some Laplanders are Swedish. So some Laplanders are not Chinese.

3 Derive a valid conclusion that follows only from all three premises together: Feathers of the moa bird cannot be had at any price. Nothing is sold in discount stores except what can be bought cheaply. Nothing that cannot be had at any price can be bought cheaply.

4 Derive a valid conclusion using all these premises: Anyone likely to cause trouble in cramped quarters is dangerous aboard a space capsule. Infants are always noisy. All distracting companions are likely to cause trouble in cramped quarters. No one who would be dangerous aboard a space capsule is suitable as an astronaut for the trip to Mars. Any noisy person is a distracting companion.

5 No scientists are both bureaucrats and astronauts. All astronauts are scientists. So some astronauts are not bureaucrats.

6 Any Mexican speaks Russian or speaks Spanish. No Russian speakers are either Mexicans or Spanish speakers. So all Mexicans speak Spanish.

7 All high-performance cars that are economical are unsafe. Some economical cars are either high-performance cars or unsafe. So some economical cars are unsafe.

8 Every Cypriot is either Turkish or Greek. There are non-Turkish Cypriots. So some non-Turkish Cypriots are Greek.

9 Would you advise a person who wants to become a doctor to enroll at Calvin Coolige College? Its rules require that: All students must take logic; all premedical students must take physics; no one may take physics without taking calculus; only those who do not take calculus may take logic.

10 Anyone who knows either Jan or Dora knows Ken. No one who knows both Jan and Dora knows Ken. So no one who knows Jan knows Dora.

†B Analyze the following arguments.

1 Speculative opinions...and articles of faith...which are required only to be believed, cannot be imposed on any church by the law of the land. For it is absurd that things should be enjoined by laws which are not in men's power to perform. And to believe this or that to be true does not depend upon our will.   JOHN LOCKE, *A Letter Concerning Toleration*

2 Philosophy must possess complete certitude. For since philosophy is a science, its content must be demonstrated by inferring conclusions with legitimate sequence from certain and immutable principles. Now, that which is inferred by legitimate sequence from certain and immutable principles is thereby certain and cannot be doubted....Hence, since there is no room for doubt in philosophy, which is a science, it must possess complete certitude.

CHRISTIAN WOLFF, *Preliminary Discourse on Philosophy in General*

3 Some...have...expressed themselves in a manner...of imagining the whole of virtue to consist in singly aiming according to the best of their judgment, at promoting the happiness of mankind in the present state; and the whole of vice in doing what they foresee, or might foresee, is likely to produce an overbalance of unhappiness in it: than which mistakes, none can be conceived more terrible. For it is certain, that some of the most shocking instances of injustice, adultery, murder, perjury, and even of persecution, may, in many supposable cases, not have the appearance of being likely to produce an overbalance of misery in the present state; perhaps sometimes may have the contrary appearance.

JOSEPH BUTLER, *The Analogy of Religion*

4 The governments, not only the military ones, but the governments in general, could be, I do not say useful, but harmless, only in case they consisted of infallible, holy people....But the governments, by dint of their very activity, which consists in the practice of violence, are always composed of elements which are the very opposite of holy,—of the most impudent, coarse, and corrupted men. For this reason every government...is a most dangerous institution in the world.

LEO TOLSTOI, "Patriotism and Government"

5 The senses never give us anything but instances, that is to say particular or individual truths. Now all the instances which confirm a general truth, however numerous..., are not sufficient to establish the universal necessity of this same truth.... Whence it seems that necessary truths...must...not depend upon instances, nor, consequently, upon the witness of the senses...   LEIBNIZ, *New Essays*

CHAPTER 3

THE LOGIC OF TRUTH FUNCTIONS

In this chapter we shall study a group of deductive arguments quite different in character from those based on categorical sentences. These arguments will contain compound sentences of a special kind, and will depend for their validity upon the special properties of these sentences.

11 ARGUMENTS CONTAINING COMPOUND SENTENCES

We may think of an argument as having two parts. One part consists of those words which make up its logical skeleton, that is, its logical form, or structure. The other part consists of those words which are the flesh with which the skeleton is filled out. For instance, (1) is an argument, and (2) is its logical skeleton:

All spiders are eight-legged. (1) No wasps are eight legged. ——————————————— ∴ no wasps are spiders.	All...are ### (2) No *** are ### ——————————— ∴ no *** are...

In argument (1) the words "all," "no," and "are" make up the logical skeleton, while the words "spiders," "wasps," and "eight-legged" are the flesh with which the skeleton happens to be clothed. Notice that (1) is a valid argument, and it is valid *because* (2) is a valid kind of skeleton. That is, *any* argument having this same form will have a true conclusion provided that its premises are true.

All the arguments dealt with in Chapter 2 were like (1) in that their logical skeletons had gaps that were to be filled by single words or phrases. However, not all arguments are like this. Consider argument (3) and its skeleton (4):

This is a wasp, or this is a spider.   (3)   ### or...   (4)
This is not a wasp.   Not ###

──────────────────────────────   ──────────

∴this is a spider.   ∴....

Argument (3) is deductively valid too, but notice the difference between skeleton (4) and skeleton (2). The gaps in (4) must be filled not by single words or phrases but by whole sentences. In argument (3) the sentences which happen to fill these gaps are the sentences "This is a wasp" and "This is a spider." Notice also that in analyzing this argument we must think of the first premise not as a categorical sentence but rather as a compound sentence. Only by thinking of it in this way can we see what makes the argument valid. We shall now become acquainted with some of the main kinds of arguments that contain compound sentences like this—arguments whose fleshy parts are whole sentences.

Some of them are very simple, trivial forms of argument. You may think that they are pointless or silly. But remember that simple arguments can be combined to form chains of reasoning, and a chain of reasoning may succeed in reaching an interesting conclusion that was not obvious, even if each step in it is trivial and obvious.

Negation

A simple way of forming a compound sentence is by adding at the beginning the words "It is not the case that." The sentence "It is not the case that spiders are insects" is a compound sentence, for it contains within itself the simpler sentence "Spiders are insects." We say that the former sentence is the *negation* of the latter sentence. The negation of a given sentence is *contradictory* to it; that is, it denies just what the given sentence says, no less and no more.

Another way of forming negations is to use the single word "not." "Spiders are not insects" also expresses the negation of "Spiders are insects." But notice that the word "not" is somewhat unreliable as a way of forming negations. "Some spiders are not insects" fails to be the negation of "Some spiders are insects," because these sentences are not contradictories. The negation of the latter sentence is best expressed as "It is not the case that some spiders are insects," and is equivalent to "No spiders are insects."

The negation of a sentence will deny just what the sentence says, no less and no more. Therefore, the negation of the negation of a sentence will have to be equivalent to the original sentence itself. This provides us with two extremely simple forms of argument that involve negation only.

Double negation

Not (not p)	e.g. It is not the case that wasps aren't insects.
$\therefore p$	Therefore wasps are insects.
p	e.g. Wasps are insects.
$\therefore$ not (not p)	Therefore it is not the case that wasps aren't insects.

Here, in representing the forms of compound sentences, we have stopped using cumbersome dots, asterisks, and so on; instead, we use the letters "p," "q," and "r," which are to be thought of as doing just the same job—that is, marking places where whole sentences may be filled in. We shall use capital letters when we wish to abbreviate specific sentences—thus we can let "W" be short for "Wasps are insects," and then the two examples we were just considering of double-negation arguments can be abbreviated "not (not W), $\therefore$ W" and "W, $\therefore$ not (not W)."

Notice, however, that we cannot use the principle of double negation to cancel out negations indiscriminately. From "It is not the case both that there will not be rain and that there will not be snow," we are not entitled to infer "There will be rain, and there will be snow." The structure of this mistaken reasoning is:

Not (not p and not q)

$\therefore$ p and q

This is a misuse of the principle of double negation. Here the mistake is that our premise is the negation of an "and" sentence rather than the negation of a negation. To avoid mistakes like this, we need to pay close attention to the logical forms of the expressions with which we deal. The position of a negation can make a great difference to its meaning.

As another example, we have to distinguish among:

Not (p or q)	e.g. It is not the case that it will either rain or snow.
Not p or q	e.g. It will not rain, or it will snow.
Not p or not q	e.g. It will not rain, or it will not snow.

Here are three different forms of sentences which say three different things. They are not equivalent.

Disjunction

A compound sentence consisting of two simpler sentences linked together by "or" (or by "either...or...," which means just the same) is called a *dis-*

junction (or an *alternation*). A disjunction is symmetrical, in the sense that "*p* or *q*" always is equivalent to "*q* or *p*." We can rewrite our earlier skeleton (4) using letters:

Disjunctive arguments

p **or** *q*	also: *p* **or** *q*	e.g. It will rain, or it will snow.
Not *p*	Not *q*	It will not rain.
∴ *q*	∴ *p*	∴ it will snow.

These forms of disjunctive arguments are valid because the first premise tells us that at least one component is true, while the second premise tells us that a certain component is not true. It follows that the other component must be true.

In English there are two different ways of using the word "or." Sometimes when we say "*p* or *q*," what we mean is "*p* or *q* but not both." This is called the *exclusive* sense of "or." More often when we say "*p* or *q*," we mean "*p* or *q* and perhaps both." This is the *nonexclusive* sense of "or." In ordinary conversation, if a gentleman says to his girlfriend in a tone of acquiescence, "I'll buy you a Cadillac, or I'll buy you a mink coat," he is surely using "or" in the nonexclusive sense, since one cannot accuse him of having spoken falsely if he then gives her both. Cases of the exclusive sense of "or" occur, though less often. If a father says to his child in a tone of refusal, "I'll take you to the zoo, *or* I'll take you to the beach," then one can accuse him of having spoken falsely if he takes the child both places.

It seems best to adopt the policy of always interpreting the word "or" in the nonexclusive sense except in those cases where we have some positive indication that the exclusive sense is intended. In this way, we can be sure of not taking too much for granted. Therefore, we regard the following two forms of argument as invalid:

Invalid disjunctive arguments

p or *q*	*p* or *q*	e.g. He's guilty, or she's guilty.
p	*q*	He's guilty.
∴ not *q*	∴ not *p*	Therefore she's not guilty.

These forms would be valid if "or" were understood in the exclusive sense, but they are invalid when "or" is understood in the commoner, nonexclusive sense.

Conjunction

A compound sentence consisting of two simpler sentences linked by the word "and" is called a *conjunction*. Sometimes, as in the sentence "They got married and had a baby," the word "and" may mean "and then," indicating that one event occurred first and the other event occurred later. But other times, as in the sentence "I like cake, and I like candy," the word "and" is simply used to join together two assertions, without indicating any time relationship. This latter sense of "and" is what we are concerned with. When "and" is used in this minimum sense, conjunctions are symmetrical; that is, "p and q" is equivalent to "q and p." In English, various other words, such as "but" and "although," often do essentially the same logical job as "and." One absurdly simple but perfectly valid form of conjunctive argument is this:

Valid conjunctive argument (simplification)

p and q	Also: p and q	e.g. It rains, and it snows.
∴ p	∴ q	∴ it rains.

If we combine negation with conjunction, we can obtain a slightly less trivial kind of valid conjunctive argument:

Valid conjunctive arguments

Not (p and q) p	e.g. Sue and Kim don't both smoke. Sue smokes.
∴ not q	∴ Kim doesn't smoke.

Not (p and q) q	e.g. Jon and Tim aren't both poor. Tim is poor.
∴ not p	∴ Jon isn't poor.

The following forms are invalid, however:

Invalid conjunctive arguments

Not (p and q) Not p	e.g. Mac isn't both young and wise. Mac isn't young.
∴ q	∴ Mac is wise.

Not (p and q) not q	e.g. Sue doesn't both fish and ride. Sue doesn't ride.
∴ p	∴ Sue fishes.

Conditionals

Consider the sentence, "If tufa floats, then some rocks float." This is a compound sentence consisting of two simpler sentences, "Tufa floats" and "Some rocks float", linked by the words "if" and "then". In order for this compound sentence to be true, the simpler sentences do not necessarily have to be true. Thus, someone who asserts the compound sentence is not committed to believing that tufa floats, or that some rocks float. What such a person is committed to is the claim that the truth of "Tufa floats" would be sufficient to ensure that "Some rocks float" is true. To put it another way, such a speaker is claiming that tufa doesn't float unless some rocks float.

A sentence consisting of two simpler sentences linked by the words "if" and "then" (or just by "if") is called a *conditional* sentence, or a *hypothetical* sentence. The part to which the word "if" is directly attached is called the *antecedent* of the conditional sentence, and the other part is called the *consequent*. Let us consider some forms of arguments containing conditional sentences.

Modus ponens

If p then q	e.g. If tufa floats, some rocks float.
p	Tufa floats.
∴ q	∴ some rocks float.

Modus tollens

If p then q	e.g. If French is easy, Italian is easy.
Not q	Italian isn't easy.
∴ not p	∴ French isn't easy.

Somewhat similar, but not deductively valid, are the following:

Fallacy of affirming the consequent

If p then q	e.g. If profits rise, taxes rise.
q	Taxes rise.
∴ p	∴ profits rise.

Fallacy of denying the antecedent

If p then q	e.g. If the car runs, it has gas.
Not p	The car doesn't run.
∴ not q	∴ the car doesn't have gas.

Another valid form has three conditional sentences, the consequent of the first being the same as the antecedent of the second:

Chain argument (or hypothetical syllogism)

If p then q	e.g. If Fido barks, Rover barks.
If q then r	If Rover barks, Champ barks.
∴ if p then r	∴ if Fido barks, Champ barks.

We can also construct even longer chain arguments with any number of premises. The one requirement for a valid chain argument is that the consequent of the first premise must serve as the antecedent of the next, the consequent of that premise as the antecedent of the next, and so on, while the conclusion must have the first antecedent as its antecedent and the last consequent as its consequent.

Another style of argument involving a conditional premise goes by the name of *reductio ad absurdum* (Latin: "reduction to the absurd"). Suppose we want to prove that there is no largest whole number (integer). We may reason as follows: If there is an integer larger than every other integer, then (because adding 1 to it will yield a still larger integer) it is not an integer larger than every other integer. From this it follows that there is not a largest integer. This reasoning has the form:

Reductio ad absurdum

If p then not p	e.g. If there is a largest integer, then
	there is not a largest integer.
∴ not p	∴ There is not a largest integer.

This style of reasoning may seem puzzling because one may be inclined to think that a sentence of the form "if p then not p" says something impossible, something necessarily false. This is not so. A sentence of the form "if p then not p" can very well be true, but only if its antecedent is false. This is why the conclusion follows. The premise tells us that the truth of the antecedent will carry with it a consequent inconsistent with the truth of the antecedent. Thus the antecedent is 'reduced to absurdity,' and this entitles us to conclude that the antecedent is false.

Another similar way of reasoning involves reducing an antecedent to absurdity by pointing out that it can have a consequent which is necessarily false. For example:

Reductio ad absurdum (another form)

If p then both	e.g. If I get home before dark, then I'll both have
q and not q	come at 90 mph and not come at 90 mph
∴ not p	∴ I won't get home before dark.

Here the point perhaps is that I'm 90 miles from home, and it's one hour until darkness; yet if I drive on this road at 90 m.p.h. I'll surely crash. Here the premise is a conditional whose consequent is necessarily false, but this does not prevent the premise as a whole from being a true sentence. The antecedent is 'reduced to absurdity,' and this allows us to infer that it is false.

In ordinary language when we come to put a compound sentence into words the component sentences often are condensed together, to make the whole sentence more manageable. Instead of saying "Ellen is coming, and Fay is coming," we are likely to say "Ellen and Fay both are coming." Instead of saying "John is a baker, or Bill is a baker," we may say "John or Bill is a baker." The shorter sentence is clearly equivalent to the longer one in cases like this. Translations back and forth between the fuller standard form and the shorter colloquial form are easy, and we need not make a fuss about them.

EXERCISE 11

*A Abbreviate each argument using the suggested letters (keep clear what each letter means). Identify the form and say whether it is deductively valid.

1 This concerto is by Bach or by Handel. It isn't by Handel, so it must be by Bach. (B, H)

2 Cigarette smoking is a major cause of heart disease and of cancer. So it's a major cause of heart disease. (H, C)

3 If it's above zero today, my car will start. But it's not above zero today, so my car won't start. (A, C)

4 If the moon is full, the dogs all howl. If the dogs all howl, Mr. Smith calls the police. So, if the moon is full, Mr. Smith calls the police. (M, D, S)

5 The suspect wasn't both at the scene of the crime and at his mother's house. He was at his mother's. So he wasn't at the scene of the crime. (C, M)

6 Either Jack did well in math or he didn't do well in physics. He didn't do well in math. So he didn't do well in physics. (M, P)

7 It's not the case that 3 is both a real number and an imaginary number. It isn't imaginary. So it's real. (R, I)

8 If Jill is late for school, she won't learn her lessons today. She isn't going to learn her lessons today. So she will be late for school. (S, L)

9 Mary loves either her husband or son. She does love her son. So she doesn't love her husband. (H, S)

10 If this creature bites, it isn't a toad. It's not the case that it isn't a toad. So it doesn't bite. (B, T)

11 The dog is friendly, if the child approaches it quietly. The child does approach it quietly. So the dog is friendly. (F, Q)

12 If the company is to stay profitable, it must raise its prices (to increase unit revenue) and not raise its prices (to preserve market share). So the company isn't going to stay profitable. (S, R)

13 We're going to win the game. So it's not the case that we won't win. (W)

14 If I join the Navy, I'll go to sea. If I become an admiral, I'll go to sea. So if I join the Navy, I'll become an admiral. (J, S, A)

15 If it rains and freezes, then the streets will be wet and slippery. It is raining and freezing. So the streets will be wet and slippery. (Choose your own letters. How many are needed?)

16 They won't fail to come. So they will come. (C)

17 If Al doesn't sing, Tim and Bo won't dance. Al won't sing. So Tim and Bo won't dance. (Choose your own letters.)

18 It's not the case that some judges aren't lawyers. So some judges are lawyers. (Choose your own letters.)

19 If these are two different circles each going through three of the same points, then these are not two different circles each going through three of the same points. So these aren't two different circles each doing that. (T)

20 His driving licence won't have been revoked if he hasn't violated the law. But he must have violated the law, as his licence has been revoked. (V, R)

B A pundit predicts that if interest rates fall, the stock market will rise; but if interest rates don't fall either inflation will accelerate or neither will the stock market rise nor will inflation accelerate. Which of the following outcomes accord with the prediction?

1 Interest rates fall, the stock market rises, and inflation accelerates.

2 Interest rates hold steady, the stock market rises, inflation accelerates.

3 Interest rates fall, the stock market doesn't rise, inflation accelerates.

4 Interest rates don't fall, the stock market doesn't rise, but inflation accelerates.

5 Interest rates fall, the stock market rises, inflation does not accelerate.

6 Interest rates rise, the stock market rises, inflation decelerates.

7 Interest rates fall, the stock market crashes, inflation stops dead.

8 Interest rates rise, the stock market falls, inflation ceases.

12 TRANSLATING INTO STANDARD FORM; DILEMMAS

Many ordinary arguments admit of being translated into the kind of standard forms we have just been discussing. We have already noticed some ambiguities and misunderstandings that can arise when we try to interpret sentences involving negation, disjunction, and conjunction. However, translations involving them usually are comparatively straightforward. With the conditional, though, the situation is more complicated.

Consider the following ways in which a conditional may be formulated:

If he's a senator, then he's over thirty.	If p then q
if he's a senator, he's over thirty.	If p, q
He's over thirty if he's a senator.	q if p
He's over thirty provided he's a senator.	q provided p
He's a senator only if he's over thirty.	p only if q
He's not a senator unless he's over thirty.	Not p unless q
Unless he's over thirty, he's not a senator.	Unless q not p

All these sentences are equivalent to one another. In each sentence "He's a senator" may be regarded as the antecedent and "He's over thirty" as the consequent. Each of these conditional sentences claims that the antecedent expresses a sufficient condition for the consequent—his being a senator is sufficient to guarantee his being over thirty. Also, each claims that the consequent expresses a necessary condition for the antecedent—his being over thirty is necessary to his being a senator.

An important point to notice about conditionals is that "if p then q" is not in general equivalent to "if q then p." Thus, "If he's a senator, then he's over thirty" is not equivalent to "If he's over thirty, then he's a senator." These two sentences express independent thoughts, and the truth of one does not guarantee the truth of the other.

Because of this, we have to be on our guard. It is easy to make the mistake of supposing that "if" means the same as "only if"; and this would lead one to suppose that "He's a senator only if he's over thirty" means the same as "He's a senator if he's over thirty." But this is quite wrong. The general rule is that "p only if q" is always equivalent to "if p then q" but not to "if q then p."

Similarly, when we translate an "unless" sentence into "if-then" form, we must be careful to distinguish correctly between antecedent and consequent, and not get them in the wrong positions. A general rule for translating "unless" sentences is: negate either part of the "unless" sentence and make it the antecedent of your conditional. Thus, "p unless q" can become either "if not p then q" or "if not q then p." For example, "He's an admiral unless he's a general" is equivalent to "If he isn't an admiral, then he's a general" and to "If he isn't a general, then he's an admiral." But it is not equivalent to "If he's an admiral, then he isn't a general" or to "If he's a general, then he isn't an admiral."

When the antecedent and consequent trade places in a conditional sentence, we obtain what is called the *converse* of the original sentence. Thus, "If he's over thirty, then he's a senator" is the converse of "If he's a senator, then he's over thirty." In general, "if q then p" is the converse of "if p then q." As we have already noticed, the converse is a new and different sentence which need not agree with the original as regards truth and falsity.

In a conditional sentence, if the antecedent and consequent trade places and also each of them is negated, we obtain what we call the *contrapositive* of the original sentence. Thus, "If he's not over thirty, then he's not a senator" is the contrapositive of "If he's a senator, then he's over thirty." And in general, "if not q then not p" is the contrapositive of "if p then q." The contrapositive always is equivalent to the original sentence. This is because the original sentence says in effect that the truth of p ensures the truth of q, while its contrapositive says that the falsehood of q ensures the falsehood of p—which amounts to the same thing.

Understanding these relationships can help us to deal with arguments which are not stated in standard form. Suppose we are wondering about whether a given argument is valid, but as it stands, it is not in any one of our standard forms. If its premises and conclusion can be translated into equivalent sentences that do form an argument of a standard type, then we can use what we know about the validity of the standard type to evaluate the validity of the given argument. Our method here permits two sorts of moves: We may replace any premise or conclusion by a new sentence equivalent to it; and we may change the order of the premises. Such moves will have no effect on the validity or invalidity of the argument. Our aim in dealing with a non-standard argument will be to get it into some familiar standard form so that we can reliably tell whether it is valid.

For instance, we may handle an example as follows:

Mica sinks only if tufa doesn't sink. ⟶ If M then not T
Mica does sink. ⟶ M
Hence tufa doesn't sink. ⟶ Therefore not T

Here the arrows merely connect each original sentence with its translation, to indicate our moves. We use capital letters to abbreviate the sentences, and it is important always to keep clearly in mind what sentence a given capital letter is short for. (We shall not use the small letters "p," "q," and "r" to abbreviate particular sentences; they will be reserved for use when we are representing general logical forms.) The above argument is translated into a case of modus ponens, because the first premise becomes a conditional whose antecedent is the same as the second premise and whose consequent is the same as the conclusion. Since the original argument can be translated into modus ponens, we know that the original argument is valid.

Here is another example:

If argon burns, neon burns. ⟶ If X then A
If argon doesn't burn, xenon doesn't burn. ⟶ If A then N
So xenon does not burn unless neon does. ⟶ If X then N

Here we have replaced the second premise by its contrapositive, letting the double negations cancel out; this is permissible because our new sentence is strictly equivalent to the original one. Also, we have changed the order of the premises, as we are permitted to do. Since this new argument that we obtain is a valid chain argument, we know that our original argument is valid also.

We shall conclude this section by considering one further group of standard forms for arguments containing compound sentences. Arguments of this group are called *dilemmas,* and they combine conditional and disjunctive sentences in a special way.

Simple constructive dilemma

If p then q	e.g. If he gives her mink, he loves her.
If r then q	If he gives her a Rolls, he loves her.
p or r	He gives her mink or a Rolls.
∴ q	∴ he loves her.

Simple destructive dilemma

If p then q	e.g. If he graduates, he'll have passed physics.
If p then r	If he graduates, he'll have passed biology.
Not q or not r	He won't pass physics or won't pass biology.
∴ not p	∴ he isn't graduating.

Complex constructive dilemma

If p then q	e.g. If she shot intentionally, she's guilty of murder.
If r then s	If she shot unintentionally, she's guilty of manslaughter.
p or r	She shot intentionally or unintentionally.
∴ q or s	∴ she's guilty of murder or manslaughter.

Complex destructive dilemma

If p then q	e.g. If he's smart, he earned profits.
If r then s	If he's honest, he paid taxes due.
Not q or not s	He didn't earn profits or didn't pay taxes due.
∴ not p or not r	∴ he isn't smart or isn't honest.

A valid constructive dilemma is like a double use of modus ponens, while a valid destructive dilemma is like a double use of modus tollens. A dilemma is invalid if it resembles the fallacy of affirming the consequent or of denying the antecedent.

Invalid dilemma

If p then q	e.g. If he gets all the answers right, he'll pass the test.
If r then not q	If he gets all the answers wrong, he'll fail the test.
q or not q	He'll either pass or fail.
∴ p or r	∴ he'll get all the answers right or all the answers wrong.

Dilemmas have often been used by debaters, and they were a formidable weapon in the rhetoric of the ancients. Often dilemmas whose overall logical form is valid nevertheless contain logical flaws that prevent them from being good arguments (we shall return to this point in Chapter 6).

If your opponent in a debate presents a dilemma which you do not know how to find fault with but whose conclusion you do not wish to accept, then you are said to be 'caught on the horns of a dilemma.' If you succeed in showing that his argument is unsatisfactory by pointing out that the disjunctive premise is not true, then you 'escape between the horns of the dilemma.'

EXERCISE 12

*A Abbreviate each argument, using the suggested letters, translate it into some standard form, name the form, and say whether it is valid.

1 Ed knows Latin if he knows Greek. He does know Latin. So he knows Greek. (L, G)

2 Sue will perform if Rod requests it. If Jon requests it, Sue will perform. Rod or Jon will request it. So Sue will perform. (S, R, J)

3 The music is baroque if it's by Vivaldi. It's not baroque unless it's not romantic. So if the music is by Vivaldi, it's not romantic. (B, V, R)

4 Cara will drive unless she flies. She won't fly. So she'll drive. (D, F)

5 If Jack approved it, the loan was made. If Ellen approved it, the loan was made. But either Jack didn't approve it or Ellen didn't approve it. So the loan wasn't made. (J, L, E)

6 Matt will have eaten, if Jane cooked. Matt didn't eat unless Bob ate too. So Bob ate only if Jane cooked. (J, M, B)

7 The sale will not be completed unless financing is found. But the sale will be completed. So financing is being found. (S, F)

8 Jill will go running only if it isn't going to be hot. She isn't going to run. So it won't be hot. (J, H)

9 This cylinder is square only if it's both round and not round. So this cylinder isn't square. (S, R)

10 If interest rates rise, retail prices will rise. Interest rates will rise only if unemployment rises. But either retail prices won't rise or unemployment won't. So interest rates won't rise. (I, R, U)

11 If the cylinder is empty, the pump will operate. If the vapor pressure is excessive, the pump won't operate. So if the vapor pressure is excessive, the cylinder isn't empty. (C, P, V)

12 If mice sing, some rodents sing. Fleas dance only if some insects dance. Either it's not the case that some rodents sing or it's not the case that some insects dance. So either mice don't sing or fleas don't dance. (M, R, F, I)

13 Ellen will come if Bill does. Donna will come unless Chris doesn't. Either Ellen or Donna will come. So either Bill or Chris will come too. (E, B, D, C)

14 Unless clubs were not led, I can take this trick. I have a good hand if spades are trump. Either clubs were led or spades are trump. So either I can't take this trick or I have a good hand. (C, T, S, G)

15 The landlord may evict the tenant only if the tenant has not fulfilled the terms of the lease. If the rent is overdue, the tenant has not fulfilled the terms of the lease. So if the rent is overdue, the landlord may evict the tenant. (E, L, R)

B Which of the following sentences are equivalent to "If Al knows calculus, then he knows algebra"?

1 Al knows calculus only if he knows algebra.

2 Al doesn't know algebra without knowing calculus.

3 Al doesn't know algebra only if he doesn't know calculus.

4 Al knows algebra only if he knows calculus.

5 Al doesn't know calculus without knowing algebra.

6 Al doesn't know calculus only if he doesn't know algebra.

7 Al knows calculus unless he doesn't know algebra.

8 Al doesn't know algebra provided that he doesn't know calculus.
9 Al knows algebra only if he knows calculus.
10 Al knows calculus unless he doesn't know algebra.
11 Al knows calculus if he doesn't know algebra.
12 If Al doesn't know algebra, then he doesn't know calculus.
13 Al doesn't know calculus unless he knows algebra.
14 Al knows calculus if he knows algebra.
15 Al knows algebra if he knows calculus.
16 Al knows calculus unless he knows algebra.
17 Al doesn't know algebra if he doesn't know calculus.
18 Al knows calculus provided that he knows algebra.
19 Al doesn't know algebra unless he knows calculus.
20 Al doesn't know calculus unless he knows algebra.
21 Al doesn't know calculus if he doesn't know algebra.
22 Al knows algebra if he doesn't know calculus.
23 Al knows algebra unless he doesn't know calculus.
24 Al knows algebra unless he knows calculus.

13 TRUTH FUNCTIONS AND THEIR GROUPING

To say that a compound sentence is *truth-functional* is to say that whether it is true or false is strictly determined by (is a function of) the truth or falsity of the shorter sentences of which it is composed. That is, settling the truth or falsity of each of its component sentences enables us to settle whether the compound sentence is true or false. Not all compound sentences are truth-functional; for instance, in order to discover whether "Ted is going because Jim is coming" is true or whether it is false, we need to know more than just whether "Ted is going" is true and whether "Jim is coming" is true. However, most sentences of the kinds considered in the preceding section are truth-functional, and this allows us to develop further methods for testing arguments which involve such sentences.

Negation

How is a sentence that is a negation related to its component sentence? The relation is that they must be opposite as regards truth and falsity. We can use the following little table to show the relationship. Here we use the dash as our symbol for negation, writing "$-p$" as short for "It's not the case that p."

p	$-p$
True	False
False	True

This "truth table" has two lines, covering the two cases that arise here. If p is true, its negation is false (first line). If p is false, its negation is true (second line). We may interpret "*p*" as short for whatever sentence we please, and the table will show how our chosen sentence and its negation are related.

In using the dash symbol for negation, we shall always interpret the dash as governing as little of what follows as would make sense. Thus, in "–*p* and *q*" the negation sign is to be regarded as governing only "*p*," not "*p* and *q*." That is, "–*p* and *q*" means "(–*p*) and *q*" rather than "–(*p* and *q*)."

For the purposes of symbolic logic, when we speak about *the negation* of a sentence, we shall understand this in a special, restricted way. The negation of any sentence will be just that very sentence, with a negation sign written in front of it so as to apply to the whole of it. Thus, the negation of "*p*" is "–*p*", the negation of "*p* or *q*" is "–(*p* or *q*)", the negation of "–*p*" is "– –*p*", and so on.

In order to write down the negation of a given sentence, we must place our negation sign properly, and not just stick it in anywhere. If we want the negation of "*p* and *q*", for instance, we must not carelessly wrote down "–*p* and *q*", or "–*p* and –*q*". Neither of these versions is the negation of the given sentence; its negation is "–(*p* and *q*)", and these versions are not even equivalent to that.

Moreover, even if we do succeed in writing down something that is equivalent to the negation of the given sentence, we may still not have written down its negation. Thus, "– –*p*" is the negation of "–*p*", and "*p*" is equivalent to "– –*p*", but this does not make "*p*" the negation of "–*p*" (although of course "*p*" is a *contradictory* of "–*p*").

Conjunction

How is a sentence that is a conjunction related to its two component sentences? The answer is that the conjunction is true when both its parts are true, and otherwise it is false. Here too we can draw up a truth table to show the relationship. Let us use "T" to abbreviate "true" and "F" to abbreviate "false."

p	*q*	*p* & *q*
T	T	T
F	T	F
T	F	F
F	F	F

We use the ampersand as our symbol for truth-functional conjunction, writing "*p* & *q*" as short for "*p* and *q*." Our truth table needs four lines to cover the possible situations. Thus, for instance, the sentence "It will rain, and it will get colder" is true if it both rains and gets colder, but is false if either one of these things fails to happen or if both fail to happen.

As we noticed earlier, "and" is sometimes used in English to mean "and then," as in "They got married and had a baby." Such a sentence is not truth-functional. Merely knowing whether they got married and whether they had a baby does not enable you to know whether "They got married and (then) had a baby" is true—you also need to know which happened first. Since we are using the ampersand to mean just "and," not "and then," it would be misleading to symbolize "They got married and had a baby" as "M & B." However, when we are analyzing an argument, often it is all right to replace a premise that is a non-truth-functional "and" sentence by a truth-functional conjunction. The truth-functional conjunction, though it says less, may well express that part of the meaning which is relevant to the validity of the argument.

Disjunction

What is the relation between a disjunctive sentence and its component sentences? A nonexclusive disjunction is true whenever at least one of its components is true, and it is false otherwise. Here our table must have four lines, as there are four possible situations to be considered. Using the wedge as our symbol for nonexclusive disjunction, we can abbreviate "p or q" as "$p \vee q$."

p	q	$p \vee q$
T	T	T
F	T	T
T	F	T
F	F	F

Here we may replace "p" and "q" by any sentences we please, and the table will show how they are truth-functionally related to their disjunction.

Conditionals

Conditional sentences present a difficulty, because the words "if-then" are often used in ways that are not truth-functional. However, let us consider some cases where "if-then" is truth-functional.

Suppose a petulant mother exclaims, "If I've told you once, then I've told you a thousand times." She means this in a sense in which it is equivalent to denying that she has told you once without telling you a thousand times. If we write "O" for "I told you once" and "T" for "I told you a thousand times," then the mother's original remark may be expressed "If O then T." And it is equivalent to "$-(O \& -T)$." This compound sentence is false if "O" is true but "T" is false (if she told you once but did not tell you a thousand times), and it is true otherwise. Construed in this way, the sentence is truth-functional, since its truth or falsity is strictly determined by the truth or falsity of its component parts.

Let us take another example and see exactly what the truth function is which "if-then" expresses. Suppose someone says, "If the Cavaliers lose today, then I'm a monkey's uncle." What he is saying can be reworded as "It's not the case both that the Cavaliers lose today and that I'm not a monkey's uncle." We can draw up a table for this:

C	M	–M	C & –M	–(C & –M) If C then M
True	True	False	False	True
False	True	False	False	True
True	False	True	True	False
False	False	True	False	True

The four horizontal lines (rows) of this truth table represent the four possible combinations of truth and falsity for "C" and "M." Since we are dealing with specific sentences here, just one of these combinations must represent the actual situation; but we are interested in all four possibilities, for we are studying the meaning of the conditional. The first two columns of the table show these possibilities and form the starting point. In the first line, where "C" and "M" both are true, "–M" must be false. Hence "C & –M" has to be false too. Its negation "–(C & –M)" must therefore be true; and "If C then M" which means the same will be true too. In the second line, the reasoning is just the same. In the third line, since "M" is false, "–M" will be true, and "C & –M" will be true too. Thus "–(C & –M)" will be false. In the fourth line, since "C" is false, "C & –M" must be false too, and so "–(C & –M)" must be true.

What has been said in this particular case holds good in general. The rule is: a truth-functional conditional is false when its antecedent is true and its consequent false, and is true otherwise. We represent the truth-functional conditional by means of the horseshoe symbol. Thus "$p \supset q$" will be our way of writing it, and here is its truth table:

p	q	p ⊃ q
T	T	T
F	T	T
T	F	F
F	F	T

We have defined the horseshoe symbol in such a way that "$p \supset q$" has to be equivalent to "–(p & –q)." Therefore, the negation of "$p \supset q$," that is, "–(p $\supset$ q)," has to be equivalent to "p & –q." Now, you might have thought that "–(p $\supset$ q)" would be equivalent to "p $\supset$ –q." But this is not so. You see, "$p \supset q$" and "p $\supset$ –q" are not contradictories. They might both be true, as will happen when "p" is false. We can illustrate these relationships this way:

p	q	–q	p ⊃ q	–(p ⊃ q)	p & –q	p ⊃ –q
T	T	F	T	F	F	F
F	T	F	T	F	F	T
T	F	T	F	T.	T	T
F	F	T	T	F	F	T

In this table the first two columns define the starting point. The third column is an auxiliary column, to be used when we fill in the last two columns. The fourth column is for a conditional, and its four lines are filled in on the basis of the first two columns in the way we just discussed. The fifth column is for the negation of the conditional, and so in each line it must be opposite to the fourth column, as regards truth or falsity. In the sixth column we consider "p & –q," and we fill in the column by looking back at the first and third columns. It will be true when "p" and "–q" both are true (the third line), and it will be false otherwise. Now we can see that the fifth and sixth columns are alike in every line, thereby showing that "–(p ⊃ q)" and "p & –q" are equivalent—alike as regards truth or falsity in every possible case. Our last column is for "p ⊃ –q." This conditional is false when its antecedent is true and its consequent is false (first line), and is true otherwise. We can see that "p ⊃ –q" and "–(p ⊃ q)" are not equivalent, as they differ with regard to truth and falsity in the second and fourth lines.

We can draw up a truth table for a conditional only when it is a truth-functional conditional. In English, however, the words "if-then" are often (perhaps much more often) used in ways that are not truth-functional. Suppose someone says, "If you drop this vase, then it will break." The speaker means to assert *more* than merely that it is not the case that you will drop it without its breaking. Over and above this, the speaker is saying that dropping it *would cause* it to break. Here we may know the truth or falsity of the component sentences "You will drop it" and "It will break" (perhaps we agree that you are not going to drop it and that it is not going to break), and yet still we may disagree or be in doubt about the truth or falsity of "If you drop it, it will break." A conditional sentence understood in this way is not truth-functional, and we lose part of its meaning if we replace it by the weaker sentence "D ⊃ B."

However, if we make it our practice to use the truth-functional horseshoe to symbolize conditional sentences, we can usually test arguments very adequately. For the truth-functional horseshoe expresses that part of the meaning of conditional sentences which normally is important as regards the validity of arguments in which conditional sentences occur.[14]

Biconditionals

A compound sentence is called a *biconditional* when it consists of two simpler sentences linked by the words "if and only if." When these words are understood in a truth-functional sense, "p if and only if q" is symbolized "p

≡ q." Of course, "p if and only if q" is equivalent to "p if q and p only if q". That is, "p ≡ q" is equivalent to "(q ⊃ p) & (p ⊃ q)." Let us draw up a truth table for the latter expression in order to see what the truth table for the former should be.

p	q	(q ⊃ p)	(p ⊃ q)	(q ⊃ p) & (p ⊃ q)	p ≡ q
T	T	T	T	T	T
F	T	F	T	F	F
T	F	T	F	F	F
F	F	T	T	T	T

The third and fourth columns of this table are obtained from the first two columns, in light of the rule that a conditional is always true except when its antecedent is true and its consequent false. The fifth column is obtained from the third and fourth, in light of the rule that a conjunction is true when and only when both its parts are true. The last column is copied from the fifth; it shows us that the biconditional is true whenever its components are alike as regards truth and falsity, and it is false whenever they differ.

A biconditional says something stronger than does a single conditional. Thus "You'll be promoted if and only if you pass the examination" promises that passing the examination is necessary *and* sufficient for being promoted. In contrast, the single conditional "If you pass the examination, then you'll be promoted" merely says that passing the examination is sufficient, while the other conditional "You'll be promoted only if you pass the examination" merely says that passing the examination is necessary.

Summary

Looking back over what we have learned about various types of truth functions, we can formulate these rules:

A *negation* always is opposite to the sentence negated, as regards truth or falsity.

A *conjunction* is true when and only when both parts are true.

A *disjunction* is true when and only when at least one part is true.

A *conditional* is false when its antecedent is true and its consequent is false; otherwise it is true.

A *biconditional* is true when and only when its parts are alike as regards truth or falsity.

Grouping

When we deal with expressions containing several symbols, it is important to pay attention to the grouping of the parts. This is because changing the grouping of its parts sometimes can entirely change the meaning of an expression. Therefore, if we are to avoid misunderstanding when we write down truth-functional compounds, we always need to make clear what grouping is intended. We shall use parentheses for this purpose.

Notice, for instance, the difference between "p & (q ∨ r)" and "(p & q) ∨ r." The former is a conjunction, one part of which is a disjunction. The latter is a disjunction, one part of which is a conjunction. They are not equivalent, for they can differ as regards truth and falsity.

To see that this is so, suppose we replace "p" by the sentence "I'm going to Paris," and replace "q" by the sentence "I'm going to Quebec," and replace "r" by "I'm going to Rome." Suppose that in fact I am not going to Paris or Quebec but am going to Rome. Then the compound sentence "I'm going to Paris and either to Quebec or to Rome"—which is of the form "p & (q ∨ r)"—is false, since I'm not going to Paris. But the corresponding sentence, "Either I'm going both to Paris and to Quebec or I'm going to Rome"—which is of the form "(p & q) ∨ r"—is true, since I am going to Rome.

Our example shows that "p & (q ∨ r)" is not equivalent to "(p & q) ∨ r." For this reason it would be improper to write the expression "p & q ∨ r" without parentheses. This expression is ambiguous, because it might have either of two quite different meanings. One cannot tell whether it is supposed to be a conjunction, one part of which is a disjunction, or a disjunction, one part of which is a conjunction.

Carelessly written sentences in ordinary language, such as "I'm going to Paris and Quebec or Rome," are ambiguous in just the same confusing way. But if we word the sentence more carefully and use a comma, the meaning can be made clear. Thus, "I'm going to Paris, and I'm going to Quebec or Rome" has the logical structure "p & (q ∨ r)." And "I'm going to Paris and Quebec, or to Rome" has the logical structure "(p & q) ∨ r." In addition to the comma and other forms of punctuation, we can use pairs of words such as "both-and" and "either-or" to prevent ambiguity and make our meanings clear.

EXERCISE 13

A For each pair of formulas: (a) Is the first the negation of the second? (b) Is the second the negation of the first? (c) If neither is the negation of the other, are they nevertheless contradictories?

1. −q; q
2. −−r; r
3. −−r; −r
4. −−−p; −−p
5. p & q; −p & q
6. −(p & q); p & q
7. p ⊃ q; −(p ⊃ q)
8. p ⊃ q; p ⊃ −q
9. −p ⊃ q; −(−p ⊃ q)
10. q ∨ r; −q ∨ −r
11. p ∨ q; −(q ∨ p)
12. r ⊃ q; −q ⊃ −r
13. −(r & q); q & r
14. p ≡ q; −p ≡ q
15. q ∨ r; −q ∨ r
16. −(p ⊃ q); p ≡ q

17. $p \equiv q; -(p \equiv q)$ **18.** $p; -(p \lor q)$
19. $p \mathbin{\&} (q \lor r);$ **20.** $(q \supset p) \mathbin{\&} (p \supset q);$
    $-p \mathbin{\&} -(q \lor r)$ $-[(q \supset p) \mathbin{\&} (p \supset q)]$

B Let "W" mean "It gets warmer," let "M" mean "The snow melts," and let "O" mean "The sun comes out." Match each sentence of the first group with the one from the second group that most closely corresponds to it.

Group I

1 If it doesn't get warmer, the snow doesn't melt.
2 It's not the case that it gets warmer, or the snow melts.
3 It gets warmer if and only if the snow melts.
4 It gets warmer only if the snow melts.
5 It's not the case that the snow melts if it gets warmer.
6 Neither does it get warmer nor does the snow melt.
7 It's not the case either that it gets warmer or the snow doesn't melt.
8 It's not the case that it gets warmer if and only if the snow melts.
9 Unless it doesn't get warmer, the snow doesn't melt.
10 It's not the case both that it gets warmer and the snow melts.
11 It gets warmer if and only if the snow doesn't melt.
12 It's not the case both that it doesn't get warmer and the snow melts.
13 It gets warmer or the snow doesn't melt.
14 It gets warmer unless the snow melts.
15 It doesn't get warmer and the snow doesn't melt.

Group II

1. $W \supset M$	**2.** $W \supset -M$
3. $-W \supset M$	**4.** $-W \supset -M$
5. $-W \lor M$	**6.** $W \lor -M$
7. $-W \mathbin{\&} -M$	**8.** $W \equiv M$
9. $W \equiv -M$	**10.** $-(W \lor M)$
11. $-(W \lor -M)$	**12.** $-(W \mathbin{\&} M)$
13. $-(-W \mathbin{\&} M)$	**14.** $-(W \equiv M)$
15. $-(W \supset M)$	

C Letting "W" and "M" mean the same as before, and letting "O" mean "The sun comes out," match each sentence from the first group with its closest kin in the second group.

Group I

1 It gets warmer, only if the snow melts and the sun comes out.
2 If the sun comes out, it gets warmer and the snow melts.
3 If it gets warmer the snow melts, and the sun comes out.
4 It gets warmer, or the sun comes out if the snow melts.
5 If it gets warmer, then the snow melts only if the sun comes out.
6 If it gets warmer only if the snow melts, then the sun comes out.
7 It gets warmer, and the snow melts if and only if the sun comes out.
8 It gets warmer, if and only if the sun comes out if the snow melts.
9 The sun comes out, if either it doesn't get warmer or the snow doesn't melt,
10 It's not the case that, if it gets warmer, either the snow melts or the sun comes out.

11 If it gets warmer if and only if the snow melts, then the sun comes out.

12 It gets warmer if and only if both the snow melts and the sun comes out.

13 Either the snow melts or the sun doesn't come out, if it doesn't get warmer.

14 That it gets warmer only if the snow melts, is the case if and only if the sun comes out.

15 It's not the case that if either it doesn't get warmer or the snow melts, the sun comes out.

Group II

1. $W \equiv (M \& O)$
2. $W \& (M \equiv O)$
3. $(W \supset M) \& O$
4. $(W \supset M) \equiv O$
5. $W \supset (M \supset O)$
6. $(W \equiv M) \supset O$
7. $W \supset (M \& O)$
8. $W \equiv (M \supset O)$
9. $-[W \supset (M \lor O)]$
10. $-[(-W \lor M) \supset O]$
11. $(W \supset M) \supset O$
12. $O \supset (W \& M)$
13. $W \lor (M \supset O)$
14. $(-W \lor -M) \supset O$
15. $-W \supset (M \lor -O)$

D Let "A" be short for "Australia is not in Africa," let "B" be short for "Bulgaria is in Europe," let "M" be short for "Manila is in China,", and let "N" be short for "New Delhi is in Russia." Determine whether each sentence is true.

1. $A \& B$
2. $A \& M$
3. $M \lor N$
4. $M \lor B$
5. $A \supset B$
6. $M \supset N$
7. $A \supset M$
8. $A \equiv B$
9. $B \equiv N$
10. $M \lor -N$
11. $-(N \equiv A)$
12. $-(M \supset A)$
13. $A \& (M \& B)$
14. $M \lor (N \lor A)$
15. $M \lor (M \supset N)$
16. $N \lor (M \equiv N)$
17. $A \supset (M \supset B)$
18. $N \supset (M \& -A)$
19. $-N \supset (-M \lor -B)$
20. $-M \& (A \lor N)$
21. $N \lor (B \supset -A)$
22. $-[A \supset (M \lor N)]$
23. $-B \equiv -(A \& N)$
24. $-[(M \supset A) \supset B]$

E Let "C" mean "Canada is larger than England," let "D" mean "Denmark is smaller than India," let "O" mean "Omaha is the capital of Spain," and let "P" mean "Philadelphia is in Cuba." Determine whether each sentence is true.

1. $(C \& D) \lor (O \& P)$
2. $(O \lor P) \& (C \lor D)$
3. $(C \& D) \supset (O \& P)$
4. $(O \lor P) \supset (D \lor C)$
5. $C \supset [D \lor (O \& P)]$
6. $(O \supset C) \lor (P \supset D)$
7. $(D \supset P) \supset (C \& O)$
8. $(O \equiv C) \supset (P \equiv D)$
9. $(O \& P) \equiv -(C \lor D)$
10. $(D \equiv O) \supset (P \& O)$
11. $(C \supset P) \& (D \lor O)$
12. $-[P \supset (C \& D)] \supset O$
13. $[(C \& C) \lor (O \& P)] \lor D$
14. $(O \lor -O) \supset [(D \& C) \& P]$
15. $(O \supset -O) \supset [P \supset (C \lor D)]$
16. $(P \& -P) \supset [(C \lor D) \supset D]$
17. $(C \lor -C) \supset [(O \& -O) \& D]$
18. $(O \supset C) \& [D \equiv (P \& D)]$
19. $-(O \& P) \supset -[C \& (D \lor P)]$
20. $-[(P \& C) \lor (O \& C)] \& D$
21. $[(O \equiv P) \& (C \equiv D)] \lor D$
22. $(P \equiv C) \supset [(D \equiv O) \lor P]$
23. $-[O \& (P \equiv C)] \equiv (P \supset B)$
24. $P \supset -[(C \lor O) \& (D \equiv P)]$

14 TRUTH TABLES

In light of the rules concerning truth functions that we learned in the preceding section, we shall be able to construct truth tables for more complex sentences—truth tables that will enable us to answer several kinds of logical questions.

A complete truth table for a compound sentence must have lines representing all possible cases—all the different combinations of truth and falsity that could arise for its basic component sentences. The number of possible situations that must be considered (the number of horizontal lines in the truth table) depends on the number of different basic components.

In the second section of this chapter we wrote a truth table for "$-p$," which needed only two lines. Similarly, a truth table for "$(p \lor -p)$ & p" would need only two lines. Where only one basic component is present (in this case there is only "p"), the only possibilities to be considered are its truth and its falsity. However, a truth table for "$p \lor q$" has to have four lines, and so does a truth table for "$(q$ & $p) \lor (q \lor p)$." Here "p" and "q" are the basic components. Thus "p" may be either true or false when "q" is true, and may be either true or false when "q" is false, making four possibilities. If we were dealing with a compound containing three different basic components, there would be eight possibilities to consider and so eight lines in the truth table. In general, each additional basic component doubles the number of lines required in the truth table.

In constructing a truth table, we need to be sure to take account of just the proper possibilities; using a systematic procedure will help. In drawing up the initial columns, let us follow the practice of alternating the entries in the first column ("T" in the first line, "F" in the second line, etc.), pairing the entries in the second column ("T" in the first and second lines, "F" in the third and fourth lines, etc.), alternating by fours the entries in the third column, and so on.

When we are dealing with complicated compounds, it often helps to use auxiliary columns, working step by step to reach the final column in which we are interested. For instance, suppose we want a truth table for "$(r$ & $q) \supset (p \equiv r)$." Since this contains three basic components, we require eight lines. The compound as a whole is a conditional, one part of which is a conjunction and the other part a biconditional. Here it will be wise to use two auxiliary columns, one for the conjunction and one for the biconditional. Then it will be easier to draw up the final column for the conditional as a whole. The table will look like this:

p	*q*	*r*	*r & q*	*p ≡ r*	*(r & q) ⊃ (p ≡ r)*
T	T	T	T	T	T
F	T	T	T	F	F
T	F	T	F	T	T
F	F	T	F	F	T
T	T	F	F	F	T
F	T	F	F	T	T
T	F	F	F	F	T
F	F	F	F	T	T

Here three initial columns have been drawn up in a systematic fashion so as to take account of exactly the right possibilities. The fourth and fifth columns are auxiliary columns drawn up by looking at the first three columns. Then from the fourth and fifth columns we get the sixth column, the one we are seeking. The sixth column tells us, in each of the eight possible cases, whether the compound is true or false. From the table we obtain the information that the compound is false only if "p" is false and "q" and "r" are both true.

Logicians have also devised various other methods for working out the answers to questions about truth-functional compounds. Some of them yield their answers more quickly and with less writing than this truth-table method does. But this truth-table method has the advantage of being easy to explain and to understand.

Truth-Functional Implication and Validity

When one sentence (or group of sentences) implies another and the relationship depends solely upon the truth-functional forms of the sentences concerned, we call this a *truth-functional implication*. Truth tables provide a method for telling whether truth-functional implications hold. The method is this: we construct a truth table containing a column for each sentence involved in the implication. Then we inspect the table line by line to see whether there is any line in which the supposedly implying sentences are all true and the supposedly implied sentence is false. If there is such a line, then the implication does not hold. If there is no such line, the implication does hold.

An argument whose premises truth-functionally imply its conclusion is said to be *truth-functionally valid*. We can use a method similar to the one above for telling whether an argument is truth-functionally valid. We construct a truth table containing a column for each premise of the argument and a column for the conclusion. Then we inspect the table line by line to see whether there is any line in which all the premises are true and the conclusion is false. If there is such a line, the argument is not truth-functionally valid; otherwise it is.

All valid arguments of the forms discussed in the first section of this chapter are truth-functionally valid. Each of them can be shown to be truth-functionally valid in this way. As an example, let us consider modus ponens. A truth table for a particular argument of this form will contain columns for the two premises, say, "A ⊃ B" and "A" and a column for the conclusion "B." Or we can make the headings more general in style by expressing the premises as "p ⊃ q" and "p" and the conclusion as "q." When we do it this latter way, the understanding is that the truth table represents *any* argument of this form.

Premise p	Conclusion q	Premise p ⊃ q
T	T	T
F	T	T
T	F	F
F	F	T

Since just two basic letters occur in the argument, we need four lines in the table; we have a column for each premise and one for the conclusion. Now, what does the table show? We see that the first line is the only line in which both premises are true, and in the first line the conclusion is true too. There is no possibility of having the premises all true and the conclusion false. This demonstrates that the premises truth-functionally imply the conclusion, that is, that modus ponens is truth-functionally valid.

As another example, let us consider arguments of the form "p, therefore p v q." This is a simple type of disjunctive argument which we have not discussed so far; it is called *disjunctive addition*.

| Premise | | Conclusion |
p	q	p v q
T	T	T
F	T	T
T	F	T
F	F	F

Here the table shows that whenever "p" is true, "p v q" must be true also, and so this form of argument is valid. Of course, it is a very trivial form of argument. Someone who argued "It is raining; therefore it is raining or snowing" would not be offering us interesting food for thought. However, the argument is strictly valid, and it might be of value as one step in the middle of some longer chain of reasoning.

As another example, let us treat the simple destructive dilemma. Can we show by means of a truth table that this form of argument is valid? Here we need columns for the premises "p ⊃ q," "p ⊃ r," and "–q v –r," and we need a column for the conclusion "–p." Since there are three letters, the table must have eight lines. The work is easier if we use some auxiliary columns to help us reach the final ones.

p	q	r	Premise p ⊃ q	Premise p ⊃ r	–q	–r	Premise –q v –r	Concl. –p
T	T	T	T	T	F	F	F	F
F	T	T	T	T	F	F	F	T
T	F	T	F	T	T	F	T	F
F	F	T	T	T	T	F	T	T
T	T	F	T	F	F	T	T	F
F	T	F	T	T	F	T	T	T
T	F	F	F	F	T	T	T	F
F	F	F	T	T	T	T	T	T

Here the fourth and fifth columns are for the first two premises, and we get them from the three initial columns by using the rule for the conditional. The sixth and seventh columns are auxiliary ones taken from the initial columns by using the rule for negation. The eighth column is for the third premise, and we derive it from the sixth and seventh, using the rule for disjunction. Then we add a column for the conclusion. Inspection of the completed table shows that only in the fourth, sixth, and eighth lines are all premises true, and in each of these lines the conclusion is true. Hence the table shows this form of argument to be truth-functionally valid.

As a final example of this procedure, let us consider the particular argument:

If matter exists, Berkeley was mistaken.
If my hand exists, matter exists.
Therefore, either my hand exists or Berkeley was mistaken.

We may symbolize it:

$M \supset B$
$H \supset M$
$\therefore H \vee B$

Let us test the validity of this argument by means of a truth table.

M	B	H	Premise $M \supset B$	Premise $H \supset M$	Conclusion $H \vee B$
T	T	T	T	T	T
F	T	T	T	F	
T	F	T	F		
F	F	T	T	F	
T	T	F	T	T	T
F	T	F	T	T	T
T	F	F	F		
F	F	F	T	T	F

We are concerned only with the question whether it is possible for the premises both to be true and the conclusion false, and so any parts of the table that do not help to answer that question may be left blank. Thus we leave the fifth column blank in the third and seventh lines, for we are interested only in lines where both premises are true. We leave the last column blank in the second, third, fourth, and seventh lines for the same reason. The eighth line finally gives a definite answer to our question, for in that line both premises are true and the conclusion is false. This demonstrates that the argument is not truth-functionally valid.

Truth-Functional Equivalence

To say that two sentences are equivalent to one another is to say that they necessarily are alike as regards truth and falsity. When they are equivalent simply because of their truth-functional form, we say that they are *truth-*

functionally equivalent. Truth tables provide a method for determining whether sentences are truth-functionally equivalent. Consider a sentence of the form "–(p & q)" and a corresponding sentence of the form "–p & –q." Are these truth-functionally equivalent? We can establish the answer by constructing a truth table containing a column for each compound. Then we compare these columns, line by line. If they are alike in every line, this shows that the equivalence holds, while if the columns differ in any line, the equivalence does not hold. (Notice that it would not make sense to say that the compounds are equivalent in some lines but not in others. Being equivalent means being alike as regards truth and falsity in *all* possible cases.)

Continuing with this example, let us draw up a table with a column for each of the two compounds. Let us also include a column for "–p ∨ –q" so that it can be compared with the others.

p	*q*	*p & q*	*–(p & q)*	*–p*	*–q*	*–p & –q*	*–p ∨ –q*
T	T	T	F	F	F	F	F
F	T	F	T	T	F	F	T
T	F	F	T	F	T	F	T
F	F	F	T	T	T	T	T

Here the third column is obtained from the first two and serves as an auxiliary column from which we get the fourth column. The fifth and sixth columns come from the first and second; from them we obtain the seventh and eighth. With the table complete, we look at it line by line, and we observe that in the second and third lines "–(p & q)" differs from "–p & –q," the former being true and the latter false. This shows that these two compounds are not truth-functionally equivalent to one another. However, "–(p & q)" and "–p ∨ –q" are just alike in each line, which shows that they are equivalent. Thus "–(p & q)" and "–p & –q" are not equivalent, while "–(p & q)" and "–p ∨ –q" are.

Not only is "–(p & q)" equivalent to "–p ∨ –q," but also "–(p ∨ q)" is equivalent to "–p & –q," as could be shown by another truth table. These two equivalences are known as *De Morgan's laws,* after the nineteenth-century logician De Morgan.

All the various equivalences mentioned earlier in this chapter also can be demonstrated by means of truth tables. We can show by truth tables that "*p*" and "–(–p)" are equivalent, that "p & q" and "q & p" are equivalent, that "p ⊃ q" and "–q ⊃ –p" are equivalent, and so on.

When two sentences are truth-functionally equivalent, each implies the other, and so either may be validly inferred from the other. This is one way in which knowing about equivalences can help us to understand certain kinds of steps in reasoning.

Another slightly more complicated principle concerning truth-functional equivalence also is useful in connection with reasoning. This principle may be illustrated as follows: A sentence of the form "r ⊃ –(p & q)" has to be equivalent to a corresponding sentence of the form "r ⊃ (–p ∨ –q)," because these two compounds are exactly alike except that where the first contains the component "–(p & q)" the second contains "–p ∨ –q," which is equivalent to it. Since the two short compounds are necessarily alike as regards truth and falsity, replacing one by the other in the longer expression cannot alter the truth table for the longer expression. Hence the altered longer expression necessarily agrees with the original longer expression, as regards truth and falsity. This principle holds in general: Any two longer truth-functional compounds are bound to be equivalent if they are exactly alike except that in one of them a component present in the other has been replaced by something equivalent to that component.

Tautology and Contradiction

When we draw up a truth table for a truth-functionally compound sentence, usually we find that it comes out true in some lines and false in other lines. But occasionally we meet extreme cases: for instance, we may meet a compound that comes out true in every line of its truth table. Such a compound is called a *tautology*. Also, occasionally we meet a compound that is false in every line of its truth table. Such a compound is a truth-functional *contradiction*. (Notice the difference between a contradiction, an expression that is bound to be false, and contradictories, sentences that are necessarily opposite in truth or falsity.)

A sentence that is a tautology is bound to be true in every possible situation. Thus, it is a kind of necessarily true sentence, whose necessary truth results from its truth-functional form. One well-known type of tautology has the form "p ∨ –p." This is sometimes called the "law of excluded middle," because it reflects the fact that any given sentence must be either true or false, there being no third alternative. Another well-known type of tautology has the form "–(p & –p)." This is sometimes called the "law of contradiction," because it reflects the fact that a sentence cannot be both true and false. Some other tautologies that do not have special names are "p ⊃ p" and "p ≡ p." There are an unlimited number of tautologies, for we can always keep inventing longer and longer ones.

A sentence that is a truth-functional contradiction is necessarily false, because of its truth-functional form. Some examples are "p & –p," "–(p ∨ –p)," and "p ≡ –p." And there are an unlimited number of other truth-functional contradictions.

To every valid truth-functional argument there corresponds a conditional that is a tautology. The conditional will have as its antecedent the conjunction of the premises of the argument, and it will have as its consequent the conclusion of the argument. For example, the tautology "[(p ⊃ q) & p] ⊃ q" corresponds to modus ponens.

To say that a form of argument is valid is to say that if its premises are true, then its conclusion must be true. Under such circumstances the corresponding conditional cannot have a true antecedent and a false consequent, and so will necessarily be true, a tautology. Thus we can say that a truth-functional argument is valid if and only if its corresponding conditional is a tautology. Hence, another way of testing the validity of a truth-functional argument would be to form a conditional whose antecedent is the conjunction of the premises and whose consequent is the conclusion, and draw up a truth table for the conditional. If the conditional is a tautology, this shows that the argument is valid; if not, the argument is invalid. However, the method described in the preceding section is slightly simpler.

EXERCISE 14

*A In each case, use a truth table to show whether the argument is truth-functionally valid.

   1 Cows moo, and horses whinny. So horses whinny.
   2 Cows moo, and horses whinny. So cows moo, or horses whinny.
   3 If horses whinny, cows moo. So if cows don't moo, horses don't whinny.
   4 If cows moo, horses whinny. So cows moo if horses whinny.
   5 Horses whinny if and only if cows moo. So cows moo if horses whinny.
   6 Cows moo, and horses whinny. So horses whinny if and only if cows moo.
   7 Horses whinny if and only if cows moo. So horses whinny and cows moo.
   8 It's not the case both that cows moo and horses whinny. So it's not the case that either horses whinny or cows moo.
   9 Horses don't whinny and cows don't moo. So, if horses whinny, cows moo.
  10 Horses whinny, or cows don't moo. So it's not the case that cows moo if horses whinny.

B In each case, use a truth table to show whether a sentence having the first form would truth-functionally imply a sentence having the second form.

1. p & q; q	**2.** q; q ∨ p
3. p & r; p ∨ r	**4.** p; q ∨ q
5. p; p ⊃ p	**6.** p ⊃ p; p
7. q; q ≡ q	**8.** q ≡ q; q
9. p ∨ q; p ⊃ q	**10.** p & q; p ⊃ q
11. −p; p ⊃ q	**12.** −p; p ≡ p
13. −(p ∨ q); −q	**14.** −(p & q); −q
15. −(p ⊃ q); p	**16.** −(p ⊃ q); −q
17. p & q; p ≡ q	**18.** p ∨ q; p ≡ q
19. p ∨ q; p & q	**20.** p ≡ q; p ⊃ q

C In each case, use a truth table to show whether a pair of sentences having the given forms would be truth-functionally equivalent.

1. p; p ∨ p	**2.** p & p; p
3. p; p ⊃ p	**4.** p ≡ p; p

5. p ∨ q; q ∨ p   **6.** p & q; q & p

7. p; p ∨ q   **8.** p & q; q

9. p ⊃ q; q ⊃ p   **10.** p ≡ q; q ≡ p

11. p & –q; q & –p   **12.** p ∨ –q; –p ∨ q

13. –(p ∨ q); –p ∨ –q   **14.** –(p & q); –p & –q

15. –p & –q; –(p ∨ q)   **16.** –p ∨ –q; –(p & q)

17. p ⊃ –q; –(p ⊃ q)   **18.** p ≡ –q; –(p ≡ q)

19. –(p ≡ q); (p & –q) ∨ (–p & q)   **20.** –(p ⊃ q); p & –q

D Which of the following are tautologies, which are truth-functional contradictions, which are neither?

1. p   **2.** p & –p

3. q ∨ –q   **4.** q ∨ q

5. p ⊃ p   **6.** –p ⊃ –p

7. q ⊃ –q   **8.** p ≡ p

9. p ≡ q   **10.** p ∨ q

11. –(p & –p)   **12.** p ⊃ (p ∨ q)

13. p & (q & –p)   **14.** p ⊃ (p ∨ p)

15. p ∨ (q ⊃ q)   **16.** q ≡ –q

17. (p & q) ⊃ q   **18.** (p ≡ –p) & q

19. (p & –p) ∨ q   **20.** (p & –p) ∨ (q & –q)

†E Which statements are true, which are false? Explain each answer.

1 The negation of any truth-functional contradiction is a tautology.

2 The negation of any tautology is a tautology.

3 The disjunction of any tautology with itself is a tautology.

4 Any disjunction, one component of which is a contradiction, is a tautology.

5 Any conjunction, one component of which is a contradiction, is a contradiction.

6 The disjunction of any sentence with itself is equivalent to the given sentence.

7 The conjunction of any sentence with a contradiction is equivalent to the given sentence.

8 Any truth-functional conditional whose antecedent is a tautology is a tautology.

9 Any truth-functional conditional whose consequent is a tautology is a tautology.

10 The conjunction of any sentence with itself is equivalent to the given sentence.

11 Any tautology is implied by any sentence.

12 Any truth-functional contradiction implies any sentence.

13 The disjunction of any tautology with any truth-functional contradiction is a contradiction.

14 Any argument whose conclusion is a tautology is valid.

15 Any argument all of whose premises are tautologies is valid.

15 FORMAL DEDUCTIONS

Truth tables provide a perfectly general method for testing the validity of all truth-functional arguments. However, when an argument is a lengthy one, and especially if it contains many different basic components, the truth-table method may be long and tedious. It is valuable to have a short-cut method to deal more efficiently with longer, more complex arguments. We shall now develop a method that involves breaking up long arguments into simpler steps (this method will also be useful in Chapter 4 in connection with another type of problem). If we can show how it is possible to pass, by means of simple valid steps, from the premises to other sentences that follow from them, and then from these to the conclusion, we shall have succeeded in showing that the conclusion does follow validly from the original premises.

Suppose we have the argument: "If he is both vacationing at Sun Valley this year and buying a Porsche, then he has inherited money. He will have inherited money only if his rich grandmother has died. He is buying a Porsche, but his grandmother is hale and hearty. Therefore, he is not vacationing at Sun Valley." Since this argument contains four different basic component sentences, its truth table would require sixteen lines and would be rather tedious. Let us try to pass to the conclusion from the premises by familiar steps. Writing "S" for "He vacations at Sun Valley," "P" for "He buys a Porsche," "I" for "He inherits money," and "G" for "His rich grandmother has died," we can symbolize our starting point as follows:

1 $(S \& P) \supset I$ Premise
2 $I \supset G$ Premise
3 $P \& -G$ Premise

We can make a useful first move by separating one part of the conjunction of line 3:

4 $-G$ From 3 by *conjunctive simplification*

Next we can put together lines 4 and 2 by using modus tollens:

5 $-I$ From 2, 4 by *modus tollens*

Then we can use modus tollens again:

6 $-(S \& P)$ From 1, 5 by *modus tollens*

And from this we can get the desired conclusion:

7 P From 3 by *conjunctive simplification*
8 $-S$ From 6, 7 by *conjunctive argument*

Here we have broken up the involved argument into a particular sequence of simple valid steps. Thus we succeed in showing that the conclusion follows from the premises. When arranged in a coherent order like this, the steps are said to constitute a deduction. Each line in the deduction must either be a premise or be clearly justified by means of some standard principle. We call it a *formal deduction* when the rules are strictly observed and no steps are permitted except the ones explicitly sanctioned by the rules.

In more advanced studies of symbolic logic, it is usual to select some very small group of standard principles for justifying steps and then to insist upon using no others. In that way, greater elegance and economy are achieved, thereby enhancing the theoretical interest of the deductions that are constructed. For our elementary purposes, however, that sort of elegance is not so important. Let us therefore include among our principles for use in deduction all those principles with which we have so far become acquainted, and also a few new ones. This broad though inelegant approach will mean that our deductions will be comparatively easy to construct; it will spare us some of the irritation sometimes felt by beginners using elegantly economical deductive rules when they find that certain moves, which they see to be perfectly valid, nevertheless are not directly sanctioned by their rules.

Let us arrange our principles under three headings. First are our standard elementary forms of valid argument; we always may write any new line in a deduction if that new line follows from earlier lines by one of these forms of argument. Next are equivalences; we always are justified in adding a new line if it is equivalent to some preceding line. Finally, we shall draw up a short list of especially useful forms of tautology, and we shall allow ourselves to add as a new line any sentence having one of the forms on our list. Tautologies have to be true, and cannot lead us astray. The underlying idea is that adding a tautology to your set of premises cannot ever change the set of conclusions that are implied by those premises.

Truth-Functional Principles for Use in Deduction

Elementary forms of valid argument

Modus ponens:	$p \supset q$, p; therefore q
Modus tollens:	$p \supset q$, $-q$; therefore $-p$
Chain argument:	$p \supset q$, $q \supset r$; therefore $p \supset r$
Disjunctive arguments:	$p \vee q$, $-p$; therefore q
	$p \vee q$, $-q$; therefore p
	p; therefore $p \vee q$ (*disjunctive addition*)
	q; therefore $p \vee q$ (*disjunctive addition*)
Conjunctive arguments:	$-(p \ \& \ q)$, p; therefore $-q$
	$-(p \ \& \ q)$, q; therefore $-p$
	$p \ \& \ q$; therefore p (*simplification*)
	$p \ \& \ q$; therefore q (*simplification*)
	p, q; therefore $p \ \& \ q$ (*adjunction*)
Reductio ad absurdum:	$p \supset -p$; therefore $-p$
	$p \supset (q \ \& \ -q)$; therefore $-p$

Dilemmas: $p \supset q, r \supset q, p \lor r$; therefore q
$$\qquad\qquad\qquad (simple\ constructive)$$
$p \supset q, p \supset r, -q \lor -r$; therefore $-p$
$$\qquad\qquad\qquad (simple\ destructive)$$
$p \supset q, r \supset s, p \lor r$; therefore $q \lor s$
$$\qquad\qquad\qquad (complex\ constructive)$$
$p \supset q, r \supset s, -q \lor -s$; therefore $-p \lor -r$
$$\qquad\qquad\qquad (complex\ destructive)$$

Equivalences Any expression may validly be inferred from any other that is equivalent to it, according to the following principles:

"p" and "$p \lor p$" and "$p \& p$" all are equivalent.
"$p \supset q$" and "$-p \lor q$" and "$-(p \& -q)$" all are equivalent.
"$p \equiv q$" and "$(q \supset p) \& (p \supset q)$" are equivalent.
"$-(p \supset q)$" and "$p \& -q$" are equivalent.

Double negation:	"p" and "$--p$" are equivalent.
Contraposition:	"$p \supset q$" and "$-q \supset -p$" are equivalent.
Commutation:	"$p \lor q$" and "$q \lor p$" are equivalent.
	"$p \& q$" and "$q \& p$" are equivalent.
Association:	"$p \lor (q \lor r)$" and "$(p \lor q) \lor r$" are equivalent.
	"$p \& (q \& r)$" and "$(p \& q) \& r$" are equivalent.
Distribution:	"$p \& (q \lor r)$" and "$(p \& q) \lor (p \& r)$" are equivalent.
	"$p \lor (q \& r)$" and "$(p \lor q) \& (p \lor r)$" are equivalent.
De Morgan's laws:	"$-(p \lor q)$" and "$-p \& -q$" are equivalent.
	"$-(p \& q)$" and "$-p \lor -q$" are equivalent.
Exportation:	"$(p \& q) \supset r$" and "$p \supset (q \supset r)$" are equivalent.

Tautologies The following list includes a number of forms of tautologies. Our rule will be that any sentence having one of these forms may be written down as a new line in a formal deduction.

$p \lor -p$	$-(p \& -p)$
$p \supset p$	$p \equiv p$
$p \supset (p \lor q)$	$(p \& q) \supset p$
$(p \& -p) \supset q$	$p \supset (q \lor -q)$

When we want to write down a tautology as a new line, we must of course make sure that it conforms *exactly* to one of these forms. We shall limit our list to just these eight forms.[15]

This list of principles perhaps looks tediously long, but the advantage of having a good many principles is that they make deductions easier to construct; all the principles in this list are standard logical principles worth being acquainted with. We have already met the elementary valid forms of argument; if any of them seems strange or dubious, its validity can be proved by means of truth tables. Disjunctive addition and conjunctive adjunction are new principles. We did not discuss them earlier because they are so absurdly simple that they don't look like serious forms of argument at all—but they can provide useful steps in formal deductions. Under the heading of equivalences are some principles that we have met and also some new ones. If any of these seems strange or dubious, again truth tables can be used. (It is also illuminating to invent sentences illustrating these principles.)

Notice that our forms of valid argument are to be used only for deriving one whole line from other whole lines in the deduction, not from parts of lines. For example, by disjunctive addition from "p" we may derive "$p \vee q$," where these occupy whole lines. But suppose we have a line which is of the form "$p \supset r$." It would be a misuse of the rules to rewrite this, replacing "p" in it by "$p \vee q$," thus obtaining a new line of the form "$(p \vee q) \supset r$." This does not follow and is not the right way to apply the rule.

The situation is different with regard to principles of equivalence, however. These may be applied to whole lines or to parts of lines. For instance, if we have a line of the form "$p \vee q$," we may use the principle of commutation to derive "$q \vee p$," thus dealing with the line as a whole. But also from a line of the form "$r \supset (p \vee q)$" we may obtain "$r \supset (q \vee p)$" by commutation, dealing with only part of the line. The underlying justification of this is that two longer truth-functional compounds have to be equivalent if they are alike except that where one contains a certain part the other contains something else equivalent to it. Equivalence of the parts to each other guarantees that the entire compounds will be equivalent to each other.

In constructing our deductions, let us try to proceed in a strict manner, always using one and only one of our principles to justify each line that we write down. In considering whether a particular move is or is not an exact instance of one of our principles, we should ask whether there is some way of getting the instance from the principle by replacing each letter in the principle ("p," "q," "r," etc.) wherever it occurs by some sentence or other, simple or compound. It is permissible to put the same sentence for more than one letter; thus, from "$(A \& B) \supset (C \vee D)$" and "$(C \vee D) \supset (A \& B)$" it would be all right to derive "$(A \& B) \supset (A \& B)$" by the principle of the chain argument—here the same thing has replaced both "p" and "r" in the principle of the chain argument, but this is permissible.

Now let us examine another example of a deduction in which more of these principles are employed. Let us suppose that we are given an argument having three premises, which we shall symbolize as lines 1, 2, and 3, and a conclusion, "C," to be derived through a deduction (we do not know at first that the conclusion will be the thirteenth line; we know that only after finishing the deduction).

1. $A \vee (B \& C)$ Premise
2. $A \supset D$ Premise
3. $D \supset C$ Premise

4. $A \supset C$ *From 2, 3 by chain argument*
5. $-- A \vee (B \& C)$ *From 1 by equivalence of "p" to " $--$ p"*
6. $- A \supset (B \& C)$ *From 5 by equivalence of " $-$ p $\vee$ q" to "p $\supset$ q"*
7. $- C \supset -A$ *From 4 by contraposition*
8. $- C \supset (B \& C)$ *From 7, 6 by chain argument*
9. $(B \& C) \supset C$ *Tautology*
10. $(B \& C) \supset -- C$ *From 9 by equivalence*
11. $- C \supset -- C$ *From 8, 10 by chain argument*
12. $-- C$ *From 11 by reductio ad absurdum*
13 C *From 12 by double negation*

In constructing the deduction, our strategy could have been the following: Looking at the premises, we see that the second and third can be put together to form a chain argument, yielding line 4. Wondering how to combine line 4 with anything else, we notice that line 1 might possibly combine with line 4. If line 1 is rewritten as a conditional instead of a disjunction, it will be more likely to combine with line 4, and so we make use of the fact that "–p $\vee$ q" is equivalent to "p $\supset$ q." Now, if line 4 is replaced by its contrapositive, we obtain a standard chain argument whose conclusion is line 8. This is close to what we want, but we still need to separate out the "C" which is contained in the consequent of line 8. If we choose an appropriate tautology, we can do this; and so we write line 9 and then get line 11 by another chain argument. Line 11 gives the desired conclusion by way of *reductio ad absurdum*. However, this is not the only way of getting from these premises to this conclusion (for instance, a shorter, more elegant deduction can be constructed using a simple constructive dilemma).

In order to construct a proof such as this, we must use a little ingenuity; we have not mastered any mechanical method that will automatically tell us what steps we should take to get from premises to conclusion. But if we are familiar with the main types of elementary forms of valid argument, with the main types of equivalences, and with simple sorts of tautologies, we find that only very little ingenuity is required to proceed step by step.

Some tactics that often are useful are these: Try working backward from the conclusion, seeking lines that the conclusion could be derived from. Always be alert for opportunities to apply modus ponens, modus tollens, disjunctive arguments, or the chain argument. Often when you have a conjunction, it is helpful to break it up by conjunctive simplification. When you have a negated conditional, it usually is wise to rewrite it as a conjunction making use of the fact that "–(p $\supset$ q)" is equivalent to "p & –q."

EXERCISE 15

*A In each of the following deductions the first two lines are premises. State the justification for each of the other lines that are not premises. Say what specific principles are used, and what earlier lines, if any, are involved.

1	1. $A \supset B$		**2**	1. $B \vee (A \ \& -C)$
	2. $C \supset A$			2. $-B$
	3. $C \supset B$			3. $A \ \& -C$
	4. $-B \supset -C$			4. $-C$
3	1. $A \ \& \ B$		**4**	1. $(E \ \& \ F) \ \& \ D$
	2. $B \supset C$			2. $(E \ \& \ F) \supset H$
	3. B			3. $E \ \& \ F$
	4. C			4. H
5	1. $C \supset A$		**6**	1. $(E \vee F) \supset (A \ \& \ B)$
	2. $-(A \ \& \ B)$			2. $-(A \ \& \ B)$
	3. $-A \vee -B$			3. $-(E \vee F)$
	4. $A \supset -B$			4. $-E \ \& -F$
	5. $C \supset -B$			5. $-F$
7	1. $G \supset -H$		**8**	1. $K \vee (C \supset K)$
	2. $-G \supset K$			2. $-K$
	3. $G \vee -G$			3. $C \supset K$
	4. $-H \vee K$			4. $-C$
	5. $H \supset K$			5. $-C \ \& -K$
9	1. $(A \supset B) \ \& \ (C \supset D)$		**10**	1. $H \supset J$
	2. $-B \vee -D$			2. H
	3. $-A \vee -C$			3. J
	4. $-C \vee -A$			4. $J \supset (J \vee K)$
	5. $C \supset -A$			5. $J \vee K$

*B Construct deductions to establish validity.

1. $-K \ \& -J, K \vee H, \therefore H$
2. $J \ \& \ K, -(K \ \& \ H), \therefore -H$
3. $-E \vee F, G \supset E, \therefore G \supset F$
4. $A \ \& \ D, C \vee C, \therefore D \ \& \ C$
5. $C \supset D, -D \supset D, \therefore D$
6. $J, A \supset K, -(K \ \& \ J), \therefore -A$
7. $-H \vee J, -J \vee -J, \therefore -H$
8. $A \supset B, A \supset -B, \therefore -A$
9. $J \supset K, -(H \ \& -H) \supset -K, \therefore -J$
10. $A, C \supset D, -(D \ \& \ A), \therefore -C$

C Construct deductions to establish validity.

1. $E \supset J, -J \supset -H, -(-H \ \& -E), \therefore J$
2. $B \supset (A \ \& -A), C \supset B, \therefore -C$
3. $-A \supset D, B \vee B, -D, \therefore (B \ \& \ A) \vee (B \ \& \ D)$
4. $(K \vee -K) \supset -J, (E \ \& \ F) \supset J, \therefore -E \vee -F$
5. $G \supset (K \ \& \ J), -(H \vee H), (J \ \& \ K) \supset H, \therefore -G$
6. $-C \supset -D, C \supset D, -C \supset -A, C \supset A, \therefore D \equiv A$
7. $-(D \vee -E) \equiv -F, F, \therefore E \supset (D \vee G)$
8. $H \ \& \ H, K \supset -K, -(G \ \& \ H), \therefore -(G \vee K)$
9. $E \supset D, -B \supset -D, B \equiv A, \therefore E \supset A$
10. $(E \ \& \ F) \supset G, H \supset E, \therefore F \supset (H \supset G)$

D Symbolize each argument, using the suggested letters. Then construct a deduction to show that it is valid.

1. If the patient had no fever, then malaria was not the cause of his illness. But malaria or food poisoning was the cause of his illness. The patient had no fever. Therefore, food poisoning must have caused his illness. (F, M, P)

2. The centrifuge is to be started if the specimen remains homogenous. Either the specimen remains homogeneous, or a white solid is precipitated. A white solid is not being precipitated. So the centrifuge is to be started. (C, S, W)

3. Had Franklin D. Roosevelt been a socialist, he would have been willing to nationalize industries. Had he been willing to nationalize industries, this would have been done during the Depression. But no industries were nationalized during the Depression. Hence Roosevelt must not have been a socialist. (R, W, D)

4. If either the husband or the wife paid the premium that was due, then the policy was in force and the cost of the accident was covered. If the cost of the accident was covered, they were not forced into bankruptcy. But they were forced into bankruptcy. Therefore, the husband did not pay the premium that was due. (H, W, P, C, B)

16 THE INDIRECT METHOD; SHOWING INVALIDITY

In this section we shall supplement our method of truth-functional deduction, first by considering an alternative way of arranging deductions, and then by noting a short-cut way of establishing that an argument is invalid.

The Indirect Method of Deduction

The method of formal deduction which we have been considering is a 'direct' method: in establishing the validity of an argument, the deduction starts from the premises and moves directly toward the conclusion. However, there is another way of organizing deductions which also is worth noticing. This is the 'indirect,' or *reductio ad absurdum*, approach. It proceeds by showing that a contradiction can be deduced from the combination of the premises with the negation of the conclusion. Let us see how this would work. Suppose we have the argument "A, $A \equiv B$, $C \supset -B$, therefore $-C$." Let us construct a deduction whose premises are the premises of the original argument plus the negation of its conclusion. Then let us try to deduce an outright contradiction from this set of assumptions. Such a deduction can be drawn up as follows:

1. A	Premises	
2. $A \equiv B$	Premises	
3. $C \supset -B$	Premise	
4. $--C$	Premise	
5. C	From 4 by double negation	
6. $-B$	From 5 and 3 by modus ponens	

7. $(B \supset A) \& (A \supset B)$ *From 2 by equivalence*
8. $A \supset B$ *From 7 by simplification*
9. $-A$ *From 8 and 6 by modus tollens*
10. $A \& -A$ *From 1 and 9 by adjunction*

What this deduction shows is that an obvious contradiction of the form "p & −p" follows from the combined four premises of the deduction. This means that those four premises cannot all be true; if the first three are true, then the fourth cannot be. But the fourth was the negation of the conclusion of our original argument, while the first three were the premises of our original argument. So what we have shown is that if the premises of the original argument are true, then the conclusion of the original argument cannot be false. This establishes that the original argument is valid.

In general, then, if we want to set up a deduction using this *reductio ad absurdum* method, we proceed as follows: Suppose that what we want to show is that a certain sentence q follows validly from certain other sentences $r_1 \ldots r_n$. We take as our premises $r_1 \ldots r_n$ together with the negation of q. And the conclusion of this deduction should be some outright contradiction, preferably of the most obvious form, "p & −p." If we can construct such a deduction, getting by valid steps from such premises to such a conclusion, then we shall have succeeded in showing that q does follow validly from $r_1 \ldots r_n$.

This indirect method is usually no better or quicker for handling truth-functional arguments than is the direct method. However, if you have trouble figuring out how to complete a direct deduction, it may be worthwhile to try constructing your deduction in this indirect style instead; sometimes an indirect deduction is easier to put together.

Showing Invalidity

Naturally, the method of formal deduction, whether direct or indirect, will work only for arguments that are deductively valid. If an argument is not valid, of course it will not be possible to construct a deduction that moves step by step from the premises to the conclusion. But the fact that we have failed to construct a deduction for an argument by no means demonstrates that it is invalid; perhaps we have not worked intelligently enough. Suppose we work on an argument, trying unsuccessfully to construct a deduction for it; we may eventually suspect that perhaps the argument is not valid. In such a situation we could resort to a truth table. But it is valuable also to have a short-cut method of demonstrating that an argument is invalid.

To say that an argument is invalid is to say that it is possible for the premises all to be true yet the conclusion false. This gives us the clue to a short-cut method of demonstrating invalidity. If we can find a way of assigning truth and falsity to the constituent letters so that the premises all will be true but the conclusion false, this will demonstrate that the argument is invalid (or, at any rate, that it is not valid in virtue of its truth-functional form, which usually means that it is invalid; we shall discuss this point further in Chapter 8).

Suppose we have an argument whose three premises are symbolized "$A \supset (B \lor C)$," "$(C \& D) \supset E$," and "$-E$," and whose conclusion is symbolized "$-A$." We shall not be able to pass, by valid steps, from these premises to this conclusion. Let us try instead to show that the argument is invalid. We want to see whether it is logically possible for the premises all to be true and the conclusion false. If the conclusion is false, "A" must be true; if "A" is true, then either "B" or "C" (or both) must be true in order that the first premise be true. Also, in order that the third premise be true "E" must be false; if "E" is false, "C" and "D" cannot both be true, in order that the second premise be true. Let us try letting "A" be true, "E" false, "B" and "C" both true, and "D" false. This proves to be one satisfactory way of assigning truth and falsity to the constituent letters, for this is a way of making the premises all true and the conclusion false. Thus we have shown that there is a logically possible way for the premises all to be true while the conclusion is false; hence the argument is shown to be invalid. This method is like finding in the truth table for the argument one single line that suffices to show that the argument is invalid.

EXERCISE 16

A Go back to part **A** or **B** of Exercise 15 and rework those formal deductions, now using the indirect method.

*B For each of the following arguments, use the short-cut method to show that it is invalid.

  1 $C \supset D, D, \therefore C$
  2 $F \lor G, F, \therefore -G$
  3 $-(A \& B), -A, \therefore B$
  4 $A \supset -B, -A \equiv B, -A, \therefore -B$
  5 $D \supset E, E \supset G, F \supset G, \therefore D \supset F$
  6 $C \supset D, -C \supset -A, -D \supset -B, \therefore -B \supset -A$
  7 $A \supset B, C \supset D, B \lor D, \therefore A \lor C$
  8 $F \supset G, H \supset K, -F \lor -H, \therefore -G \lor -K$
  9 $A \supset (C \& D), (B \lor C) \supset D, \therefore D \supset A$
  10 $K \supset (L \supset M), F \supset (G \lor H), G \supset (K \lor L), -(F \& M), \therefore F \equiv H$

C For each argument, choose an appropriate method, and show either that the argument is valid or that it is invalid.

  1 If the seal has not been broken and the routine servicing has been performed, the guarantee is in effect. The owner is responsible for the damage only if the routine servicing has not been performed or the seal has been broken. Hence, the guarantee is in effect unless the owner is responsible for the damage.

  2 Either Thales said nothing moves and Parmenides didn't say it, or else Parmenides said it and Heraclitus denied it. If Thales said it, his thought

didn't conform to the Milesian pattern. Thales' thought did conform to the Milesian pattern. Therefore, Heraclitus denied that nothing moves.

3 If either revenues increase or debt and costs decrease, the firm's profitability will improve. Costs won't decrease unless debt decreases. It's not the case both that revenues will increase and that profitability will improve. Therefore, either debts won't decrease or profitability will improve.

4 If Locke had denied the existence of spiritual substance, he would have been a materialist; if he had denied the existence of physical substance, he would have been an idealist. If he had been either an idealist or a materialist, he would not have been a dualist. But Locke was a dualist. Therefore, he did not deny the existence of either spiritual or physical substance.

5 If Moses and Abraham were patriarchs, then Samuel and Jeremiah were prophets. If Abraham was a patriarch, Samuel was a prophet. Therefore, either Moses was not a patriarch or Jeremiah was not a prophet.

D A set of sentences is consistent if and only if it is possible for all of them to be true together. You can show that a set is consistent by finding a way of assigning truth and falsity to the basic letters so as to make all the compound sentences true. You can show that a set is inconsistent by deducing a contradiction from them. Show whether sets of sentences having the following forms are consistent.

1 $p \supset q, q \supset p$

2 $p, p \supset q, -q$

3 $-(p \& q), p, q$

4 $p \lor q, -q, p$

5 $p \equiv q, q \equiv r, -(p \equiv r)$

6 $p \supset q, q \supset r, p \& -r$

7 $p \supset -q, r \supset -p, r \& -q$

8 $p \equiv (q \lor r), r \equiv -q$

9 $p \supset q, q \supset r, p \& r$

10 $p \supset (q \& r), s \supset (q \& r), s \equiv -p$

†E Analyze the structure of each of the following truth-functional arguments. Watch for unstated premises.

1 "I hope, Marianne," continued Elinor, "you do not consider Edward as deficient in general taste. Indeed, I think I may say that you cannot, for your behavior to him is perfectly cordial, and if that were your opinion, I am sure you could never be civil to him."

JANE AUSTEN, *Sense and Sensibility*

2 Murder and treachery cannot be good without regret being bad: regret cannot be good without treachery and murder being bad. Both, however, are supposed to have been foredoomed; so something must be fatally unreasonable, absurd, and wrong in the world. It must be a place of which either sin or error forms a necessary part. From this dilemma there seems at first sight no escape.

WILLIAM JAMES, "The Dilemma of Determinism"

3 With respect to every reality external to myself, I can get hold of it only through thinking it. In order to get hold of it really, I should have to be able to make myself into the other, the acting individual, and make the foreign reality my own reality, which is impossible. For if I make the for-

eign reality my own, this does not mean that I become the other through knowing his reality, but it means that I acquire a new reality, which belongs to me as opposed to him.

SÖREN KIERKEGAARD, *Concluding Unscientific Postscript*

4 Either to disinthrone the King of Heav'n
We war, if war be best, or to regain
Our own right lost: him to unthrone we then
May hope, when everlasting Fate shall yield
To fickle Chance, and *Chaos* judge the strife:
The former vain to hope argues as vain
The latter: for what place can be for us
Within Heav'n's bound, unless Heav'n's Lord supreme
We overpower? JOHN MILTON, *Paradise Lost*

5 If man lacked free judgment of will, how would that be good for which justice itself is commended when it condemns sins and honors deeds rightly done? For that which was not done by the will would be neither sinfully nor rightly done. And according to this if man did not have free will, both punishment and reward would be unjust. However, there must have been justice in both punishment and reward since it is one of the goods which are from God. Therefore, God must have given man free will.

ST. AUGUSTINE, *De Libero Arbitrio*

6 The universe, then, has no circumference, for, if it had a center and a circumference, it would thus have in itself its beginning and its end, and the universe itself would be terminated by relation to something else; there would be outside the universe another thing and a place—but all this contains no truth. NICHOLAS OF CUSA, *Of Learned Ignorance*

CHAPTER 1 - INTRODUCTION

I. LOGIC AND ARGUMENTS

A. LOGIC

LOGIC is concerned with STANDARDS OF CORRECT REASONING. Study of these standards may be done from two standpoints: FORMAL logic and NONFORMAL logic.

FORMAL logic is primarily THEORETICAL, and is concerned with a clear and systematic knowledge of the PRINCIPLES OF REASONING.

NONFORMAL LOGIC is primarily PRACTICAL, and is concerned with recognizing and avoiding COMMON MISTAKES in reasoning.

B. ARGUMENT

The notion of an ARGUMENT is fundamental to logic. As people interested in logic we want to be able to RECOGNIZE and EVALUATE arguments. We may define an argument as

> A SET OF SENTENCES CONTAINING ONE SENTENCE (CONCLUSION) WHICH IS CLAIMED TO BE PROVEN BY THE OTHER SENTENCES (PREMISES).

To understand the notion of an argument better we must first understand the notions of SENTENCE, PREMISE, and CONCLUSION.

A SENTENCE is a grammatically correct string of words which must be CAPABLE of being TRUE or FALSE. For instance, "Ancient Athens was the first democracy," is capable of being true or false. But, "Was Critias a great leader?" is not.

EXAMPLE

Which of the following are sentences according to the definition just given?
    1. Pericles was a great statesman.
    2. Bring me the vase!
    3. If it is geometric, then it is pottery from the 7th Century.
    4. Damn the Spartans!
    5. It is not the case that Pythagoras was a Greek philosopher.
    6. Which way to the Agora?

ANALYSIS

Examples 1, 3, and 5 are SENTENCES. It makes sense to say that they can be true or false.

Example 2 is a COMMAND. Commands are either obeyed or disobeyed, but they are neither true nor false.

Example 4 is an EXCLAMATION. Exclamations are neither true nor false.

Example 6 is a QUESTION. Questions themselves are neither true nor false, although the answers to questions can be true or false.

A CONCLUSION is the sentence, in an argument, which is claimed to be proven. Consider this argument:

> All men are mortal.
> Socrates is a man
> So Socrates is mortal.

Here, "Socrates is mortal," is the conclusion. It is claimed to be proven by the sentences (premises) "All men are mortal" and "Socrates is a man."

A PREMISE is any sentence in an argument which is offered as proof for the conclusion. In the argument above, "All men are mortal" and "Socrates is a man" serve as the premises.

In deciding whether a set of sentences is an argument, keep these principles in mind.

1. An argument can have only ONE CONCLUSION. If there is more than one conclusion, then there is more than one argument.
2. An argument must have AT LEAST one premise, but it may have many more.
3. We determine the premises and conclusion by the ROLE EACH PLAYS in the argument. The conclusion is always the sentence which is claimed to be proven. A premise is always a sentence which is offered as proof. Consider these arguments:

> All men are mortal   All mortals are finite.
> Socrates is a man.   Socrates is mortal.
> So Socrates is mortal.   So Socrates is finite.

In the first argument, "Socrates is mortal" is the conclusion. In the second argument "Socrates is mortal" is a premise. We can often tell which is the conclusion and which is a premise by noting certain words which may serve as CLUES or INDICATORS. For example,

CONCLUSION INDICATORS	PREMISE INDICATORS
consequently	because
therefore	since
so	as
accordingly	for
hence	inasmuch as
it follows that	otherwise
we may infer	follows from
which means that	as shown by
which shows that	as indicated by
which proves that	the reason is that

NOTE: These words do not always indicate a premise or conclusion. So we must be careful not to overestimate the value of this.

2

4. The conclusion and premises may APPEAR in ANY ORDER. For example, the "Socrates" argument might have been stated like this:
    Socrates is mortal, since all men are mortal and Socrates is a Greek.
    Here the conclusion appears first.
5. A premise or conclusion may be IMPLICIT in the argument, rather than EXPLICIT. To argue that "All men are mortal, so Socrates is mortal," is to IMPLY the premise that "Socrates is a man."
6. In any argument the person who is arguing must believe that if the premises are true, then the conclusion is true.

EXERCISE #1

A. For each statement below decide if it is a sentence. Explain your answer.

1   Homer wrote the *Iliad*. [100]
2. Was the *Odyssey* written by Hesiod? [104]
3 . By Zeus! [103]
4. Great seven Greek green. [101]
5. If the Trojans had won at Troy, there would have been no great Greek past. [105]
6. Hera was the wife of Zeus but Aphrodite was the goddess of love. [102]
7. Alcibiades, please fetch me the *Dialogues*. [126]
8. Oh, Oedipus why do you torment me so? [131]
9. Nobody pays attention to Sophocles any more. [129]
10. Ajax meant well. [127]

B. For each item, decide whether it is an argument. Explain your answer.

1. All Greeks are Europeans, and, since Parmenides is a Greek, Parmenides is European. [133]
2. The Good is distinct from the Pleasurable. For there can be such things as bad pleasures, but there can be no such things as bad goods, since bad and good exclude each other. [108]
3. If Alexander conquered Persia, then Alexander was a great soldier. And since Alexander did conquer Persia, Alexander was a great soldier. [130]
4. Zeno was not mistaken in believing that all things are motionless. For either Zeno was mistaken in believing all things are motionless or Plato was a materialist. And Plato was not a materialist. [134]
5. If Plato wrote Aristotle's *Physics,* then Greece is in Persia. [128]
6. Since Homer said it, I'll do it! [132]
7. The tragedy has the same themes as those found in the plays of Euripides. It is written in the dramatist's style. And it dates from the period in which Euripides was living. So it follows that this is a play by Euripides. [106]
8. Water is found in the soil. It is found in all living things. It makes up the sea and the clouds in the sky. And air is simply evaporated water while rocks and such are really condensed water. Therefore all things are made of water. [109]
9. People of Melos, agree with our position! - Or you will be killed! [107]
10. If Achilles gives the Tortoise a head-start in a race, then there will be some distance between the two. If there is a distance between the two, then that distance can be measured as a line. Now since a line is capable of being infinitely divided, there will be no point that can be reached that is not going to be half way between the Tortoise and Achilles. And if this is the case, then Achilles, try as he might, will never be able to overtake the Tortoise. [110]

3

II. DEDUCTIVE AND INDUCTIVE ARGUMENTS

Once we have identified an argument, including its premises and conclusion, we must then decide whether it is DEDUCTIVE or INDUCTIVE. This decision is based on the RELATIONSHIP between the PREMISES and the CONCLUSION.

A. DEDUCTIVE ARGUMENTS

In a DEDUCTIVE argument the claim is that if the premises are TRUE, then the CONCLUSION is NECESSARILY true.

EXAMPLE

Why is the following a deductive argument?
>All Athenians are Greeks.
>Some Republicans are Athenians.
>So some Republicans are Greeks.

ANALYSIS

This argument is deductive because it suggests that IF "All Athenians are Greeks," and IF "Some Republicans are Athenians," then, NECESSARILY, "Some Republicans are Greeks."

QUIZ 1

For each argument, decide whether it is deductive.

1. If *eros* is desire, then *eros* is restless. *Eros* is desire. Therefore *eros* is restless. [135]
2. I've met many Greeks. All of them were patriots. Therefore, probably, all Greeks are patriots. [137]

B. INDUCTIVE ARGUMENTS

In an INDUCTIVE ARGUMENT the claim is that if the premises are TRUE, then the conclusion is PROBABLY true, but NOT NECESSARILY true.

EXAMPLE

Why is the following argument inductive, instead of deductive.
>**Every evening so far Diogenes has put out his light and gone to sleep. It is almost evening. Diogenes will porbably put out his light and go to sleep.**

ANALYSIS

This argument is inductive because it suggests that the conclusion is PROBABLY true, based on the premises. But it leaves open the possibility that the premises are true and the conclusion is false.

QUIZ 2

For each argument, decide whether it is inductive.

1. Either Might is Right or Justice is Right. Mightis not Right. Therefore Justice is Right. [138]
2. Most Athenians in the market place are eligible to vote. Potone (Plato's sister) is an Athenian in the market place. Therefore Potone is probably eligible to vote. [136]

4

DISTINGUISHING between DEDUCTIVE and INDUCTIVE arguments may be easier, if you consider these differences.

1. In an INDUCTIVE argument, it is understood that even if the premises are true, the conclusion MAY NOT come true. In a DEDUCTIVE argument, it is claimed that if the premises are true, the conclusion MUST be true.
2. In an INDUCTIVE argument, if you go from "most" cases to a particular case, the particular case may not be proven. In a DEDUCTIVE argument, it is claimed that the premises NECESSARILY prove the conclusion.
3. In any argument where the premises say something a about "some" or "most" cases, and the conclusion says something about "all" those cases, the argument is INDUCTIVE.

EXERCISE #2

For each argument, decide whether it is deductive or inductive. Explain your answer. (At this stage you are only being asked to decide whether an argument is deductive or inductive, not whether it is good or bad.)

1. Most Athenians are lovers of democracy. Therefore, Critias, an Athenian, is probably a lover of democracy. [111]
2. After every eclipse of the moon, some calamity has struck the nation. The moon has just gone into eclipse, so some calamity will probably strike the nation. [139]
3. Pittacus is high-minded, because those who love honor are high-minded, and Pittacus loves honor. (Aristotle. *Prior Analytics*.) [113]
4. Many of the followers of Socrates are young aristocrats. So Alcibiades, a follower of Socrates, probably is a young aristocrat. [140]
5. Protagoras was a Greek and Protagoras was a sophist. Gorgias was a Greek and Gorgias was a sophist. Therefore all Greeks are Sophists. [115]
6. Each time the Persians have amassed their forces, there has been a battle. The Persians are now amassing their forces near the fields of Marathon. So tomorrow there will probably be a battle on the fields of Marathon. [112]
7. Pythagoras believed in an immortal soul; Socrates believed in an immortal soul; and Plato believed in an immortal soul. I guess all Greek philosophers believed in an immortal soul. [141]
8. The taste of wine is relative to the individual. Socrates is an individual who is tasting wine. Therefore, if the wine tastes sour to Socrates, then the wine is sour (relative) to Socrates. [114]
9. If Plato is here then Speusippus is not here. Speusippus is here. So Plato is not here [155]
10. Lately, whenever Plato is here, Speusippus is not here. Plato will be here this evening, so we shouldn't count on Speusippus being here. [142]

III. TRUTH AND VALIDITY
In logic there is a distinction between the TRUTH or FALSITY of a SENTENCE and the VALIDITY or INVALIDITY of an ARGUMENT.

A. TRUTH

To ask whether a sentence is TRUE or FALSE is to ask whether what it says is ACTUALLY the case. For example, the sentence, "Theaetetus was a man," is factually true, while the sentence, "Theaetetus could fly," is a sentence that is false.

5

B. VALIDITY

To ask whether an argument is VALID or INVALID is to ask whether it is LOGICALLY CORRECT or INCORRECT. An argument CLAIMS that the premises support the conclusion either NECESSARILY, in DEDUCTIVE arguments, or PROBABLY, in INDUCTIVE arguments. An ARGUMENT is VALID if this CLAIM is CORRECT.

In a VALID (GOOD) DEDUCTIVE argument, if the PREMISES are TRUE, then the CONCLUSION must be TRUE also. In an INVALID (BAD) DEDUCTIVE argument, the PREMISES may be TRUE, while the CONCLUSION is false.

EXAMPLE

Is the following deductive argument valid or invalid?

>All human beings are rational.
>All rational animals are featherless bipeds.
>So all human beings are featherless bipeds.

This argument is VALID. If the premises are true, then the conclusion must be true.

QUIZ 3

For each argument below, decide whether it is valid.

1. If you have a Greek ship, then you have a seaworthy ship. If you have a seaworthy ship, then you have a safe ship. Therefore if you have a Greek ship, then you have a safe ship. [143]
2. If you have a Greek ship, then you have a seaworthy ship. If you have a seaworthy ship, then you have a ship that floats. Therefore if you have a Greek ship, then you have a ship that doesn't float. [146]

In a GOOD INDUCTIVE argument, if the PREMISES are TRUE, then the CONCLUSION is AS PROBABLE as the argument claims. In a BAD INDUCTIVE argument, even if the PREMISES are TRUE, the CONCLUSION is NOT AS PROBABLE as the argument claims.

EXAMPLE

Decide whether the following inductive argument is valid.

>**I've eaten 15 olives from that jar of twenty olives, and none of them has been ripe. The next olive I eat will probably be unripe too.**

ANALYSIS

This argument is VALID since it is true, based on the evidence, that the next olive will PROBABLY be unripe. It is more likely that the olive will be unripe than that it will be ripe. Note that the argument is good even if the olive is ripe; the conclusion only was about the PROBABILITY of the next olive's being unripe.

(Inductive arguments are discussed at length in Chapter 7, so the rest of this section will be devoted to valid and invalid deductive arguments.)

To understand the difference between TRUTH and VALIDITY better, consider these points.

1. The BEST CASE for a DEDUCTIVE argument is where it is VALID and the PREMISES are TRUE. Consider this argument:

   Socrates was human. (True)
   Humans are mammals. (True)
   So Socrates was a mammal. (True)

   But this is not the only way in which an argument can be valid. Remember, a good deductive argument is one in which the conclusion MUST be true, IF the premises are true. But the premises may not be true.

2. A VALID deductive argument can have FALSE PREMISES and a FALSE CONCLUSION. Consider this argument:

   Socrates was a bird. (False)
   Birds speak Russian. (Fasle)
   So Socrates spoke Russian. (False)

   This argument is VALID because IF the PREMISES were TRUE, then the CONCLUSION WOULD HAVE TO BE TRUE.

3. A VALID DEDUCTIVE argument can have one or more FALSE PREMISES and a TRUE CONCLUSION. Consider this argument:

   Socrates was a woman. (False)
   Socrates was human. (True)
   So at least one human was a woman. (True)

   Again, IF the PREMISES were all TRUE, then the CONCLUSION would have to be TRUE also.

4. But a DEDUCTIVE argument will always be INVALID if it is possible for it to have TRUE PREMISES and a FALSE CONCLUSION. Consider this argument:

   All Greeks are Europeans. (True)
   Pericles is a Greek. (True)
   So Pericles is not a European. (False)

   This is INVALID because there is no logical connection between the premises and the conclusion. The PREMISES could be TRUE, and the CONCLUSION FALSE.

In sum, it is possible for valid and invalid arguments to have any combination of true and false premises and conclusions except the combination where the PREMISES are known to be TRUE and the CONCLUSION is known to be FALSE. (Later on we will develop powerful tools to enable us to determine the validity or invalidity of arguments in a more rigorous way.)

EXERCISE #3

Just by considering the truth or falsity of their premises and conclusions, which of the following deductive arguments can be seen to be invalid? (Assume that "T" stands for true sentences and "F" stands for false sentences.)

1. All Spartans are Greeks (T). All Greeks are rational animals (T). So no Spartans are rational animals (F). [116]
2. No Boeotians are northerners (F). All   northerners read poetry (F). So all Boeotians read poetry (F). [119]

3. All Spartans are Greeks (T). All Greeks are foreigners (F). So all Spartans are foreigners (F). [118]
4. All Spartans are fighters (T). Brasidas is a Spartan (T). So Brasidas is not a fighter (F). [120]
5. All people who read poetry are Greeks (F). All northerners are people who read poetry (F). So all northerners are Greeks (F). [117]
6. All arguments are made up of premises and a conclusion (T). All premises and conclusions are made up of sentences (T). So all arguments are made up of sentences (T). [145]
7. All Greek ships are ships that sail to sea (T). All ships that sail to sea are ships that are 2 feet long (F). So all Greek ships are ships that are 2 feet long (F). [148]
8. All citizens of Athens are persons who speak the Greek language (T). Cleon is a citizen of Athens (T). So Cleon is not a person who speaks the Greek language (F). [144]
9. All human beings are creatures who fly (T). All creatures who fly are rational animals (F). So all human beings are rational animals (T). [149]
10. Plato is Greek (T). All Greeks love olives (T). So Plato hates olives (F). [147]

IV. EMPIRICAL AND NECESSARY SENTENCES

We have seen that an argument is made up of sentences. We have seen that a good argument is one in which there is a logical connection between the truth of the premises (which are sentences) and the truth of the conclusion (which is a sentence). In terms of TRUTH and FALSITY a SENTENCE is either EMPIRICAL or NECESSARY.

A. EMPIRICAL SENTENCES

An EMPIRICAL SENTENCE REQUIRES OBSERVATION to determine whether it is true or false. For example, "Greece is on the Mediterranean" may be true or it may be false. Someone has to EXPERIENCE Greece and EXPERIENCE the Mediterranean to determine whether the sentence is true.

NOTE: The experience required need not be direct. For instance, most of us know the location of Greece from maps rather than from travel. The point is that the sentence must be CAPABLE of being established by observation (directly or indirectly), and must be knowable only on the basis of such observation.

EXAMPLE
Which of the following sentences are empirical?
1. Socrates was a man.
2. Aristophanes was a Cypriot and Aristophanes was not a Cypriot.
3. Plato had wings and could fly.
4. Either there was a man called Aristotle or there was not a man called Aristotle.

ANALYSIS
Sentences 1 and 3 are empirical. We can decide whether they are true or not ONLY if someone made the required observations. Sentence 2 will always be false, no matter what we observe. Sentence 4 will always be true, no matter what we observe.

B. NECESSARY SENTENCES

A NECESSARY SENTENCE is either ALWAYS TRUE or ALWAYS FALSE. And this truth or falsity can be determined without any observations. To decide whether a necessary sentence is true or false we must understand the sentence and determine what it means.

Some necessary sentences are NECESSARILY TRUE. For example, "A Greek is a Greek," is true by virtue of the meaning of the sentence. It is impossible for this sentence to be false.

Some necessary sentences are NECESSARILY FALSE. For example, "A Greek is not a Greek," is false by virtue of the meaning of the sentence. It is impossible for this sentence to be true.

EXAMPLE

Decide which sentences are necessarily true and which are necessarily false.
    1. If Xenophon is a philologist then Xenophon is a philologist.
    2. Socrates is both a philosopher and not a philosopher.
    3. No Pythagoreans are Pythagoreans.

ANALYSIS

Sentence 1 is necessarily true, whether we know who Xenophon is or what a philologist is. Sentences 2 and 3 are necessarily false.

EXERCISE #4

Determine whether the following sentences are examples of necessarily true, necessarily false, or empirical sentences.

1. The Parthenon is located in Athens. [150]
2. The *Republic* was and was not written by Plato. [121]
3. All things are made of earth, fire, air, and water. [153]
4. On Interpretation was written by Aristotle. [124]
5. An arrow cannot be both at rest and in motion. [122]
6. A Cretan liar is not a Cretan liar. [125]
7. If Empedocles leaps into the volcano, then Empedocles will die. [123]
8. Either Socrates was married or Socrates was not married. [152]
9. Socrates was married and he was a lifelong bachelor. [154]
10. Socrates had a wife whose name was Xanthippe. [151]

CHAPTER 2 - THE LOGIC OF CATEGORICAL SENTENCES

I. CATEGORICAL SENTENCES

A. DEFINITION OF CATEGORICAL SENTENCES

A (STANDARD-FORM) CATEGORICAL SENTENCE says something about the relationship between two CLASSES or GROUPS of things. This sort of sentence is the basic component of the SYLLOGISM. A syllogism was the major type of argument studied in traditional logic.

If you fully understand the concept of a categorical sentence, you will be able to identify a sentence's FORM, NAME, FOUR COMPONENTS, QUANTITY and QUALITY.

1. FOUR FORMS and NAMES.

Each categorical sentence has one of FOUR FORMS. And each form has a NAME.

SENTENCE	NAME	SENTENCE FORM
All artists are people.	A	All S are P
No artists are people.	E	No S are P
Some artists are people.	I	Some S are P
Some artists are not people.	O	Some S are not P

2. COMPONENTS

Each sentence has FOUR COMPONENTS.

The QUANTIFIER, "All," "No," or "Some," always occupies the first (left-most) position in the sentence: e.g., "**No** sculptures are paintings."

The SUBJECT term is a word or phrase which mentions a class of things. The subject term must include a plural noun as its principal element. The subject term occupies the second position in the sentence: "No **sculptures** are paintings."

The COPULA, "are" (in A, E, and I, sentences) or "are not" (in O sentences), connects the subject and predicate terms. It occupies the third position in the sentence: "No sculptures **are** paintings."

The PREDICATE term, like the subject term, is a word or phrase which mentions a class of things and which must include a plural noun. It occupies the fourth and final position of the sentence: "No sculptures are **paintings**."

3. QUANTITY.

In terms of QUANTITY, Categorical sentences are either UNIVERSAL or PARTICULAR.

A UNIVERSAL sentence says something about EVERY member of the subject class.

The two universal forms are

> A Sentences - "ALL pastels are crayons," says that EVERY member of the class of pastels is also a member of the class of crayons;
> E Sentences - "NO pastels are crayons," says that EVERY member of the class of pastels lacks membership in the class of crayons.

A PARTICULAR sentence only says something definite about SOME (at least one) members of the subject class.

The two particular forms are

> I Sentences -"SOME frescoes are triptychs," says that AT LEAST ONE member of the class of frescoes, but not necessarily any more than one, is also a member of the class of triptychs;
> O sentences - "SOME frescoes are NOT tryptychs," says that AT LEAST ONE fresco, but not necessarily any more than one, lacks membership in the class of triptychs.

4. QUALITY.

In terms of QUALITY, Categorical sentences are either AFFIRMATIVE or NEGATIVE.

An AFFIRMATIVE sentence says that some or all members of the subject class ARE also members of the predicate class.

The two affirmative forms are

> **A** Sentences - "ALL sonnets are poems" says that every member of the class of sonnets IS also a member of the class of poems.

> **I** Sentences - "Some sonnets ARE poems," says that at least one member of the class of sonnets IS also a member of the class of poems.

A NEGATIVE sentence says that some or all members of the subject class ARE NOT members of the predicate class.

The two negative forms are

> **E** Sentences - "NO photographs are paintings," says that NO member of the class of photographs is a member of the class of paintings.

> **O** Sentences - "Some photographs ARE NOT paintings," says that at least one member of the class of photographs IS NOT a member of the class of paintings.

EXAMPLE 1

Explain why "An apple is red" is not a categorical sentence of standard form.

ANALYSIS

There is **no quantifier** ("All," "No," or "Some").
The **subject** term ("apple") is **singular.**
The **copula** ("is") is **singular.**
The **predicate** "red" does **not** contain a **noun.**
One faithful translation of this sentence into standard form would be "All apples are red fruit."

EXAMPLE 2

Identify the name, components, quantity, and quality of the sentence, "No radical idealists are common-sense realists."

ANALYSIS

This is an **E** sentence since it has the form "No S are P."

In terms of components,

> The quantifier is "No."
> The subject term is "radical idealists."
> The copula is "are."
> The predicate term is "common-sense realists."

Its quantity is universal, since it is an **E** proposition.

Its quality is negative, since it is an **E** proposition.

QUIZ 1

For each sentence state whether it is a categorical sentence. If it is not, explain why it is not. If it is, state its name and form, components, quantity, and quality.

1. All impressionists are romantics. [210]
2. Gaugin's paintings are flat. [220]

B. VENN DIAGRAMS

A VENN DIAGRAM offers a diagram or "picture" of a categorical sentence. An empty diagram consists of two overlapping circles. One circle represents the S (subject) term. The other circle represents the P (predicate) term.

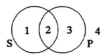

The numbers represent the regions of the diagram.

     Region 1 is for the class of things that are S but not P.

     Region 2 is for things which are both S and P.

     Region 3 is for things which are P but not S.

     Region 4 is for things which are neither S nor P.

There are three things we can do in any region when we are making a diagram to show what a sentence says.

    1. Leave the region BLANK. Do this if the sentence says nothing about that region. For example, the sentence "All architects are artists," says nothing about artists, so region 3 (P which are not S, or, in this case, artists which are not architects) is left blank when we draw a diagram for this sentence.

    2. SHADE in the region. Shading indicates that a region is VACANT. If the sentence is UNIVERSAL then it necessarily declares that a specific region is vacant. For example, the sentence, "No poems are polemics" says there is nothing which is both a poem and a polemic, so region 2 (S which are also P, or, in this case, poems which are also polemics) is being declared vacant, and should be shaded in.

    3. Place an ASTERISK (*) in the region. This indicates that there is at least one member of the class which belongs in that region. PARTICULAR propositions will be diagrammed using asterisks. For example, the sentence, "Some elegies are not eulogies," says there is at least one elegy which is not a eulogy, so region 1 (S which are not P, or, in this case, elegies which are not eulogies) should contain an asterisk.

The rules for filling in a Venn Diagram, then, are as follows:

NAME	FORM	ACTION	
A	All S are P	Shade in Region 1.	
E	No S are P	Shade in Region 2.	
I	Some S are P	* in Region 2.	
O	Some S are not P	* in Region 1.	

EXAMPLE

Draw the Venn Diagram for the sentence, "Some non-physicalists are phenomenalists."

ANALYSIS

This is an I sentence, that is, a sentence of the form "Some S are P." The correct diagram for an sentence is

Draw the Venn diagram for each sentence below.
1. Some sonatas are not chamber pieces. [230]
2. All musical works which were written for keyboard before 1700 are musical works which were not written for the piano-forte. [240]

C. DISTRIBUTION OF TERMS

TERMS, subject or predicate, are DISTRIBUTED when something is said about EVERY member of the class referred to by the term.

The S term is distributed in

A sentences: All S are P.

E sentences: No S are P.

The P term is distributed in

E sentences: No S are P

O sentences: Some S are not P

Notice that NO terms are distributed in I sentences.

EXAMPLE

Which terms are distributed in the sentence "All logical realists are non-materialists"?

ANALYSIS

This is an A sentence, that is, a sentence of the form "All S are P." Only the S term is distributed in an A sentence. The S term in this instance is "logical realists."

QUIZ 3

Identify which terms, if any, are distributed in each of the following sentences.
1. Some fugues are fantasies.[250]
2. No pedal exercises for organ are pieces played on the great manual.[260]

EXERCISE #1

A. For each sentence below decide whether it is a categorical sentence just as it stands. If it is not, explain why not. If it is, then (1) identify its name and form, its quantity, its quality, and any of its terms which are distributed; and (2) draw its corresponding Venn diagram.

1. All aesthetic judgements are not subjective. [270]
2. Some artistic experiences are not aesthetic experiences. [280]
3. Beauty is in the eye of the beholder. [290]
4. Some paintings are expressionist paintings. [2100]
5. No celestes are heard in Beethoven's Eroica. [2110]
6. Few literary works are anarchistic works. [2120]
7. Some gospel singers are opera singers. [2130]
8. No mosaics are made of bronze. [209]
9. All Etruscan art is Italian art. [219]
10. Artistic goodness is moral goodness. [229]

B. For each sentence below decide whether it is a categorical sentence. If it is not, explain why it is not. If it is, then (1) identify its name and form, its quantity, its quality, and any of its terms which are distributed; and (2) draw its corresponding Venn diagram.

15

1. All buildings in Crete during the Middle Minoan period are buildings which emphasized the king's palace rather than tombs and temples. [239]
2. The *Cupbearer in Knossos* is a fresco approximately five feet high. [249]
3. Some marble statues from the Acropolis which are now white are statues which were once painted in a variety of colors. [259]
4. No vaults that are found in churches like the Romanesque church of St. Sernin are entablatures which are supported by columns. [269]
5. Some people believe that the works of Shakespeare are actually the works of Bacon. [279]
6. Some composers whose works were enjoyed by the Nazis are not works which are still banned in Israel. [289]
7. Some paintings done by the Baroque painter Watteau are frivolous paintings depicting sculpture mixing freely with architecture on the facade. [299]
8. No piano pieces attributed to Clementi are not works that are considered less valuable than Mozart's. [2109]
9. None of Georg Kaiser's plays are plays which were meant to be performed. [2119]
10. All arias are portions of the opera which frequently are among the favorites of the audiences. [2129]

II. THE SQUARE OF OPPOSITION

A. EXPLANATION OF THE SQUARE OF OPPOSITION

The Square of Opposition shows us the SIX possible sorts of LOGICAL RELATIONSHIPS between pairs of categorical sentences which have the same subject and predicate (but different quantities and/or qualities).

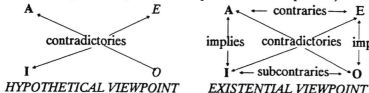

HYPOTHETICAL VIEWPOINT   EXISTENTIAL VIEWPOINT

B. CONTRADICTORIES [*A* and *O* sentences, and *E* and *I* sentences]

Sentences are contradictories if and only if
    They have the same S and P terms;
    They have different quantities;
    They have different qualities.
In terms of truth and falsity, contradictories
    CANNOT both be true;
    CANNOT both be false.
So they have to be OPPOSITE as regards TRUTH and FALSITY.

EXAMPLE

What is the contradictory of the sentence "**Some happy potters are not brain surgeons**"? If the original sentence is true, how about its contradictory? If the original sentence is false, how about its contradictory?

ANALYSIS

The original is an O sentence, thus its contradictory is an **A** sentence: **"All happy potters are brain surgeons."**

Contradictories always have opposite truth values. Thus,

If the original is TRUE, then its contradictory is FALSE;
If the original is FALSE, then its contradictory is TRUE.

QUIZ 4

For each sentence state its contradictory. If the original is true how about its contradictory? If the original is false how about its contradictory?

1. Some Persian sculptors are Greek sculptors. [208]

2. All ducal portraits in the Medici Chapel are representations of the active life and the contemplative life. [218]

C. THE HYPOTHETICAL and EXISTENTIAL VIEWPOINTS.

We have discussed contradictories. All other relationships belonging to the Square are different depending on which of TWO VIEWPOINTS is being adopted when discussing these relationships.

   1. To adopt the EXISTENTIAL viewpoint is to assume that at least one thing named by the S term exists.
   2. To adopt the HYPOTHETICAL viewpoint is to avoid making any assumption about whether or not anything exists.

EXAMPLE

Suppose we discuss the relationship between "All unicorns are horses" and "No unicorns are horses" under the assumption that at least one unicorn exists. Which viewpoint is this?

ANALYSIS

To discuss it this way is to adopt the EXISTENTIAL viewpoint, because we are making an assumption about the existence of unicorns.

QUIZ 5

In each case say which viewpoint is being adopted.

1. Without making an assumption about the existence of anything, we ask whether "All potters are people" and "No potters are people" can both be true. [2139]

2. On the basis of the assumption that there are painters, we ask whether "Some painters are protestants" and "Some painters are not protestants" can both be true. [200]

D. CONTRARIES [*A* and *E* sentences]

Two categorical sentences are contraries if and only if

They are being regarded from the existential viewpoint;
They have the same S and P terms;
They are both universal;
They have different qualities.

17

In terms of truth and falsity, contraries
> CANNOT both be true;
> CAN both be false.

EXAMPLE

What is the contrary of the sentence **"No works of art are works of craft"**? If the original is true, how about its contrary? If the original is false, how about its contrary?

ANALYSIS

This is an E sentence. The contrary of an E sentence is an A sentence. Thus the contrary is, **"All works of art are works of craft."**

Contraries cannot both be true, thus if the original is TRUE, then the contrary is FALSE.

Contraries may or may not both be false, thus if the original is FALSE, then the (truth or falsity of the) contrary is UNDETERMINED.

QUIZ 6

For each sentence state its contrary. If the original is true, how about its contrary? If the original is false how about its contrary?

1. All chromatic fantasies are difficult exercises. [228]
2. No keyboard exercises written by Bach are pieces which were designed for orchestral performances. [238]

E. SUBCONTRARIES [*I* and *O* sentences]

Two categorical sentences are subcontraries if and only if
> They are being regarded from the existential viewpoint;
> They have the same S and P terms;
> They are both particular;
> They have different qualities.

In terms of truth and falsity, subcontraries
> CAN both be true;
> CANNOT both be false.

EXAMPLE

What is the subcontrary of the sentence **"Some aesthetic objects are not physical objects"**? If the original is true, how about its subcontrary? If the original is false, how about its subcontrary?

ANALYSIS

This is an O sentence. The subcontrary of an O sentence is an I sentence, thus the subcontrary is, "Some aesthetic objects are physical objects."

Subcontraries may or may not both be true, thus if the original is TRUE, then the subcontrary is UNDETERMINED.

Subcontraries cannot both be false, thus if the subcontrary is FALSE, then the original is TRUE.

QUIZ 7

State the subcontrary of each sentence. If the original is true, how about its subcontrary? If the original is false, how about its subcontrary?

1. Some religious choral works are not works which are secular. [248]
2. Some hymns written by John Wesley's brother are hymns which are as popular today as they were when they were written almost 200 years ago. [258]

F. THE RELATIONSHIPS BETWEEN *A* and *I* AND BETWEEN *E* and *O*.

Each of these relationships holds if and only if the pair of sentences
> Are being regarded from the existential viewpoint;
> Have the same S and P term;
> Have different quantities;
> Have the same quality.

In terms of truth and falsity
> If the UNIVERSAL sentence is TRUE, then the PARTICULAR sentence is TRUE.
>> If the A sentence is true, then the I sentence is true.
>> If the E sentence is true, then the O sentence is true.
> If the PARTICULAR sentence is false, then the UNIVERSAL sentence is FALSE.
>> If the I sentence is false, then the A sentence is false;
>> If the O sentence is false, then the E sentence is false.

EXAMPLE

In terms of this relationship what is the partner of the sentence, "**Some French existentialists are playwrights**"? If the original is false, how about its partner? If the original is true, how about its partner?

ANALYSIS

This is an I sentence, so its logical partner is an A sentence: "**All french existentialists are playwrights.**"

If the particular sentence is FALSE, its partner is FALSE. Since I sentences are particular, if the I sentence is false, then the A sentence is false.

If the particular is true, its partner may be true or it may be false. Thus if this sentence is TRUE, then its partner is UNDETERMINED.

QUIZ 8

In terms of the relationship just discussed, identify the partner of each sentence below. If the oringinal is true how about its partner? If the original is false how about its partner?

1. All stories by Mark Twain are stories by Samuel Clemens. [268]

2. Some novellas are not works by Swiss authors. [278]

EXERCISE #2

A. Assume the existential viewpoint. In terms of the Square of Opposition, identify the relationship between (a) and (b). If (a) is true, how about (b)? If (a) is false, how about (b)? If (b) is true, how about (a)? If (b) is false, how about (a)?

1. (a) Some chants are dirges.

   (b) Some chants are not dirges. [288]

2. (a) No dithyrambs are choreographed works.

   (b) Some dithyrambs are choreographed works. [298]

3. (a) All plays by Sophocles are tragedies.

   (b) Some plays by Sophocles are tragedies. [2108]

4. (a) All miracle plays are plays performed on stage.

   (b) No miracles plays are plays performed on stage. [2118]

5. (a) Some auditoria are not theaters-in-the-round.

   (b) No auditoria are theaters-in-the-round. [2128]

6. (a) All reliefs on the Arch of Titus are expressionistic reliefs

   (b) Some reliefs on the Arch of Titus are not expressionistic reliefs. [2138]

7. (a) Some works by Duchamp are not Cubist works.

   (b) Some works by Duchamp are Cubist works. [207]

8. (a) Some works of art are acts of expression.

   (b) All works of art are acts of expression. [217]

9. (a) No plastic arts are performing arts.

   (b) All plastic arts are perfoming arts. [227]

10. (a) Some engravings are not etchings.

    (b) All engraving are etchings. [237]

B. For each set in Exercise A assume the hypothetical viewpoint. If (a) is true, how about (b)? If (a) is false, how about (b)? If (b) is true, how about (a)? If (b) is false, how about (a)?

   1. [247]   2. [257]   3. [267]   4. [277]   5. [287]
   6. [297]   7. [2107]   8. [2117]   9. 2127   10. [2137]

III. OPERATIONS ON CATEGORICAL SENTENCES

A. EXPLANATION OF OPERATIONS ON CATEGORICAL SENTENCES

We can perform three operations, CONVERSION, OBVERSION, and CONTRAPOSITION, on categorical sentences. These operations change the sentences into new ones. In certain cases the new sentence is related to the original in such a way that, because of their form, the two sentences are LOGICALLY EQUIVALENT to each other.

Two sentences are LOGICALLY EQUIVALENT when they NECESSARILY have the SAME TRUTH VALUE. That is, if one is true, then the other one must be true; if one is false, then the other one must be false.

Two sentences are LOGICALLY INDEPENDENT when the truth or falsity of one sentence is logically independent of the truth or falsity of the other sentence.

In considering these operations we want to know (1) how the operation is performed and (2) whether the new sentence is logically EQUIVALENT to, or logically INDEPENDENT of, the original sentence.

If we set aside conversion by limitation, then we need not distinguish the existential and hypothetical viewpoints.

B. CONVERSION

To CONVERT a sentence
> Switch subject and predicate, and
> Leave everything else the same.

The new sentence is called the **converse** of the original sentence.

In terms of logical equivalence
> An A sentence and its converse ARE NOT logically equivalent;
> An E sentence and its converse ARE logically equivalent;
> An I sentence and its converse ARE logically equivalent;
> An O sentence and its converse ARE NOT logically equivalent.

EXAMPLE

What is the converse of the sentence, "**Some columns are not fluted columns**"? Is the original logically equivalent to its converse?

ANALYSIS

To convert a proposition, switch the subject and the predicate, and leave everything else the same. The converse of this sentence is, "**Some fluted columns are not columns.**"

The original sentence is an O sentence. An O sentence and its converse are NOT logically equivalent.

QUIZ 9

State the converse of each sentence. Decide whether the original sentence and its converse are logically equivalent.

1. All quatrains are poetic stanzas. [206]
2. Some dramatic epics are not poetic pieces. [216]

C. OBVERSION

To OBVERT a sentence
> Change the quality of the sentence;
> Negate the entire predicate term, by prefixing "non" to it;
> Leave everything else the same.

The new sentence is called the **obverse** of the original sentence.

All standard-form categorical sentences are logically equivalent to their obverses.

EXAMPLE

What is the obverse of the sentence, "Some Manneristic architects are not Italian architects"? Is the original sentence logically equivalent to its obverse?

ANALYSIS

This is an O sentence. To obvert an O sentence, change the quality:
> "Some S ARE NOT P" becomes "Some S ARE P."

And negate the predicate term:
> "Some S are P" becomes "Some S are NON-P."

[NOTE: If the predicate term already is prefixed by "non" then to negate it you simply remove the "non."]

The obverse of the orignal sentence is, "Some Mannerist architects **ARE NON**(Italian architechts)." And, since all sentences are logically equivalent to their obverses, the original sentence and its obverse are logically equivalent.

QUIZ 10

State the obverse of each sentence. Are the original and its obverse logically equivalent?

1. Some pupils of Bellini are pupils of Giorgione. [226]
2. No Venetians are nonItalians. [236]

D. CONTRAPOSITION

To CONTRAPOSE a sentence

Switch the subject and the predicate;

Negate the subject and the predicate;

Leave everything else the same.

The new sentence is called the **contrapositive** of the original sentence.

In terms of logical equivalence

An **A** sentence and its contrapositive ARE logically equivalent.

An **E** sentence and its contrapositive ARE NOT logically equivalent.

An **I** sentence and its contrapositive ARE NOT logically equivalent.

An **O** sentence and its contrapositive ARE logically equivalent.

EXAMPLE

What is the contrapositive of the sentence, "**Some Fauves are French Expressionists.**" Is the original sentence logically equivalent to its contrapositive?

ANALYSIS

This is an **I** sentence. To contrapose an **I** sentence, switch the subject and the predicate:

"Some S are P" becomes "Some P are S."

And negate the subject and the predicate:

"Some P are S" becomes "Some NON-P are NON-S."

The contrapositive of the original sentence is

"Some NON(FRENCH EXPRESSIONISTS) ARE NONFAUVES."

An **I** sentence is not logically equivalent to its contrapositive, so the original sentence and its contrapositive are not logically equivalent.

QUIZ 11

State the contrapositive of each sentence below. Is the original logically equivalent to its contrapositive?

1. Some plays by Wilde are not satiric plays. [246]
2. No intaglios are works which can be done on canvas. [256]

EXERCISE #3

A. For each set of sentences below state the relationship between (a) and (b). If (a) is true, how about (b)? If (a) is false, how about (b)? If (b) is true, how about (a)? If (b) is false, how about (a)?

1. (a) All works by Klee are nonillusionistic works.
   (b) No works by Klee are illusionistic works. [266]

2. (a) No plays by Marlowe are Restoration plays.
   (b) No non(Restoration plays) are non(plays by Marlowe). [276]
3. (a) Some poems by Browning are not non(love poems).
   (b) Some non(love poems) are not poems by Browning. [286]
4. (a) Some portraits of young men are portraits painted by Boticelli.
   (b) Some non(portraits painted by Boticelli) are non(portraits of young men). [296]
5. (a) No nonmegaliths are dolmens.
   (b) All nonmegaliths are nondolmens. [2106]
6. (a) All non(rational works of art) are non(works of art by Poussin).
   (b) All non(works of art by Poussin) are non(rational works of art). [2116]
7. (a) Some non(one act plays) are not plays by Anatole France.
   (b) Some non(one act plays) are non(plays by Anatole France). [2126]
8. (a) All non(musical works) are nonpartitas.
   (b) All partitas are musical works. [2136]
9. (a) No sarabands are nonjigs.
   (b) No nonjigs are sarabands. [205]
10. (a) Some non(Dutch masters) are not Dadaists.
   (b) Some nonDadaists are not Dutch masters. [215]

B. What sequence of steps allows you to validly infer (b) from (a)? In answering consider both the Square of Opposition (assuming the existential viewpoint) and Operations on Categorical Sentences.

1. (a) No Doric capitals are Byzantine beehives.
   (b) Some Byzantine beehives are not Doric capitals. [225]
2. (a) All Suprematists are nonSurrealists
   (b) Some Surrealists are nonSuprematists. [235]
3. (a) No nonFuturists are nonFormalists.
   (b) Some nonFormalists are Futurists. [245]
4. (a) Some nonappreciators are not noncontemplators.
   (b) Some contemplators are not appreciators. [255]
5. (a) All Egyptian painters are nonConstructivists.
   (b) No Contructivists are Egyptian painters. [265]
6. (a) All nonnonobjectivists are subjectivists.
   (b) Some nonsubjectivists are not nonnonobjectivists. [275]
7. (a) Some pre-Columbians are not post-Impressionists
   (b) Some nonpost-Impressionists are pre-Columbians. [285]
8. (a) Some works of Polynesian art are works of Oceanic art.
   (b) Some works of Oceanic art are not non(works of Polynesian art). [295]
9. (a) All stage pieces are props.
   (b) No nonprops are stage pieces. [2105]
10. (a) All arches are structures.
   (b) Some structures are not nonarches. [2115]

23

IV. THE SYLLOGISM

A. DEFINITION OF THE SYLLOGISM

An argument is a (categorical) syllogism if and only if
> It contains exactly THREE standard-form categorical SENTENCES
> > (two premises and a conclusion);
> It contains no more than THREE different TERMS;
> Each of its terms appears in two different sentences.

B. MAJOR, MINOR, and MIDDLE TERMS

Consider this syllogism:
> All logicians are philosophers.
> <u>All aestheticians are logicians</u>
> So all aestheticians are philosophers.

The MAJOR term is "philosophers." It appears
> As the PREDICATE of the CONCLUSION;
> In the FIRST (MAJOR) PREMISE.

The MINOR term is "aestheticians." It appears
> > As the SUBJECT of the CONCLUSION;
> > In the SECOND (MINOR) PREMISE.

The MIDDLE term is "logicians." It appears
> In the FIRST PREMISE;
> In the SECOND PREMISE.

EXAMPLE

Is the following a categorical syllogism? If not, why not? If so, state its major, minor, and middle terms.

> **Some musicians are creative people; all composers are musicians; so some composers are creative people.**

ANALYSIS

It has exactly three standard-form categorical sentences, one of which is the conclusion (**Some composers are creative people**).

It has exactly three terms (**creative people, composers,** and **musicians**), each of which appears in two different sentences.

The predicate of the conclusion, the major Term (**creative people**), also appears in the first (major) premise.

The subject of the conclusion, the minor term (**composers**), also appears in the second (minor) premise.

The middle term (**musicians**) appears in both premises.

Therefore it is a categorical syllogism.

QUIZ 12

For each argument below decide whether it is a categorical syllogism. If it is not, explain why not. If it is, state its major, minor, and middle terms.

1. All phenomenalists are nonphysicalists. Beardsley is a phenomenalist. It follows that Beardsley is a nonphysicalist. [2125]
2. No writers of the *Sturm und Drang* era are writers of simple fiction. Some writers of simple fiction are angry people. Consequently some angry people are not writers of the *Sturm und Drang* era. [2135]

C.. MOOD

The MOOD of a syllogism is a list of the NAMES of the major premise, the minor premise, and the conclusion, in that order.

EXAMPLE

State the mood of the following syllogism.
> Some structuralists are formalists.
> <u>No formalists are materialists</u>
> Some materialists are structuralists.

ANALYSIS

The sentence containing the major term (major premise) is an **I** sentence.

The sentence containing the minor term (minor premise) is an **E** sentence.

The third sentence (conclusion) is an **I** sentence.

So the mood of this syllogism is **IEI**. Note that it would be incorrect to say that its mood is EII for we are to mention the major premise first and the minor premise second.

QUIZ 13

For each syllogism below, state its mood.

1. Some acts of perception are not scientific acts.
   <u>All acts of aesthetic perception are scientific acts</u>
   Therefore, some acts of aesthetic perception are acts of perception. [204]
2. No aesthetic objects are physical objects. This is true because all physical objects are objects requiring sense perception and no aesthetic objects are objects requiring sense perception. [214]

D. FIGURE

The FIGURE of a syllogism depends on the position of the middle term in each of the two premises.

Consider an **AAA** syllogism with the following terms:

MAJOR: good works of art
MINOR: pleasant illusions
MIDDLE: good illusions

In a FIGURE 1 syllogism the middle term is the
  SUBJECT of the MAJOR PREMISE;
  PREDICATE of the MINOR PREMISE.

All **good illusions** are good works of art.	All M are P.
All pleasant illusions are **good illusions.**	All S are M.
All pleasant illusions are good works of art.	All S are P.

In a FIGURE 2 syllogism the middle term is the
  PREDICATE of the MAJOR PREMISE.
  PREDICATE of the MINOR PREMISE.

All good works of art are **good illusions.**	All P are M.
All pleasant illusions are **good illusions.**.	All S are M.
All pleasant illusions are good works of art.	All S are P.

In a FIGURE 3 syllogism the middle term is the
  SUBJECT of the MAJOR PREMISE;
  SUBJECT of the MINOR PREMISE.

All **good illusions** are good works of art.	All M are P.
All **good illusions** are pleasant illusions.	All M are S.
All pleasant illusions are good works of art.	All S are P.

In a FIGURE 4 syllogism the middle term is the
  PREDICATE of the MAJOR PREMISE;
  SUBJECT of the MINOR PREMISE.

All good works of art are **good illusions.**	All P are M.
All **good illusions** are pleasant illusions.	All M are S.
All pleasant illusions are good works of art.	All S are P.

One way to remember the four figures is to think of an imaginary line connecting the middle terms. If this line were a baton in a cabinet, then its four positions would look like this:

| FIG 1 | FIG 2 | FIG 3 | FIG 4 |

EXAMPLE

State the mood and figure of the following syllogism.

All plays are literary works.
All literary works are nonplastic arts.
No nonplastic arts are plays.

ANALYSIS

The major premise is an A sentence. The minor premise is an A sentence. The conclusion is an E sentence. Thus the mood is AAE.

The middle term is the predicate of the major premise and the subject of the minor premise. The imaginary line connecting the middle terms looks like this:

So the syllogism is in the fourth figure.

In other words this is an **AAE-4** syllogism.

For each syllogism below state its mood and figure.

1. Some nonaesthetic portraits are descriptive portraits; no descriptive portraits are aesthetic portraits; so some aesthetic portraits are not nonaesthetic portraits. [224]
2. No onomatopoeic likenesses are nonrepresentational likenesses. Thus, no representative likenesses are nonrepresentational likenesses, since no representational likenesses are onomatopoeic likenesses. [234]

E. TESTING FOR VALIDITY USING VENN DIAGRAMS

We can test the validity of a syllogism using a Venn diagram. The test consists of THREE steps.

     1. DRAW the diagram, using THREE cirlces.
     2. DIAGRAM each premise.
     3. READ the diagram to see whether the conclusion is also diagrammed. If it is, then the syllogism is valid; if it is not, then the syllogism is invalid.

DRAWING the diagram entails drawing three intersecting circles:

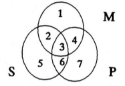

REGION: REPRESENTS THE CLASS OF THINGS WHICH ARE:

     1   M
     2   M and S
     3   M and S and P
     4   M and P
     5   S
     6   S and P
     7   P

When DIAGRAMMING the premises, follow these guidelines:

     1. If there is one universal premise and one particular premise, then DIAGRAM THE UNIVERSAL PREMISE FIRST.
     2. If, in diagramming a particular premise, you find that the asterisk could go in either of two regions then PUT A BAR ON THE LINE BETWEEN THE TWO REGIONS instead. The bar means that there is at least one thing somewhere in the region touched by the bar.

When READING the diagram, examine the circles for the S and P terms. If these circles exhibit the diagram for the conclusion, then the conclusion is valid; otherwise, the conclusion is invalid.

EXAMPLE

Use a Venn diagram to test the following syllogism for validity.

     All cinematic images are visual images.
     <u>Some cinematic images are auditory images.</u>
     So no auditory images are visual images.

ANALYSIS

We draw the circles. Then we enter the universal premise on our diagram. Then we enter the particular premise. The diagram should look like this:

Now we notice that the diagram for the conclusion, "No auditory images are visual images," is not included in the diagram for the premises. This means that when the premises are true, the conclusion does not need to be true. Therefore, this syllogism is invalid, as are all **AIE-3** syllogisms.

QUIZ 15

For each syllogism below test it for validity using a Venn diagram.

1. Some good dancers are prima ballerinas; all good dancers are mobilized statues; therefore, Some mobilized statues are prima ballerinas. [244]

2. Since some theories about metaphor are "verbal opposition theories" and since some theories about metaphor are "object comparison" theories, it follows that some "verbal opposition" theories are "object comparision" theories. [254]

EXERCISE #4

A. For each syllogism below determine its mood and figure, and test for validity using a Venn diagram.

1. Some artisans are not architects.
    All artisans are craftsmen.
    Some craftsmen are not architects. [264]

2. No mystery plays are farces.
    No farces are tragedies.
    No tragedies are mystery plays. [274]

3. All emotivists are subjectivists.
    No epiphenomenalists are emotivists.
    All epiphenomenalists are subjectivists. [284]

4. All mimes are actors.
    Some clowns are mimes.
    Some clowns are actors. [294]

5. Some speech acts are gestures.
    All gestures are physical acts.
    Some physical acts are speech acts. [2104]

6. Some literary images are mirror images.
    Some objective images are literary images.
    Some objective images are mirror images. [2114]

7. Some choreographers are not modernists.
    Some choreographers are not classicists.
    Some classicists are not modernists. [2124]

8. Some Logical Positivists are not Logical Realists.
No Logical Realists are appreciators of Baroque music.
All appreciators of Baroque music are Logical Positivists. [2134]

9. No trombonists are poets whose medium is language.
Some composers are trombonists.
Some composers are not poets whose medium is language. [203]

10. All houses are portions of Lebensraum.
No two-dimensional objects are portions of Lebensraum
No two-dimensional objects are houses. [213]

B. For each argument below decide whether it is a syllogism. If it is not, explain why not. If it is, state its mood and figure, and test it for validity using Venn diagrams.

Note: If you feel an argument is not a syllogism only because the order of the sentences is non-standard (e.g. the minor premise is stated first), change the order to make it standard, and then test for validity.

1. Things which are ugly in nature cannot become beautiful in imitation. The dead body of Jocasta is an ugly thing. Thus, the dead body of Jocasta cannot become beautiful in imitation. [223]

2. Since some people are rhetoricians, it follows that some people are technicians, since all rhetoricians are technicians. [233]

3. No sophists are philosophers. This is evident from the fact that some sophists are pioneers in seeking the answer to the question, "How are beautiful things created?" and no philosophers are pioneers in seeking the answer to the question, "How are beautiful things created?" [243]

4. Some senses are aids to harmony; some mental acts are aids to harmony, but no senses are mental acts. Thus some aids to harmony are not aids to harmony! [253]

5. Some uses of pleasure are inconsistent with the characteristics of pleasure. No uses of pleasure are antithetical to catharsis. So things which are antithetical to catharsis are inconsistent with the characteristics of pleasure. [263]

6. People who love beauty suffer from metaphysical homesickness and followers of Plotinus love beauty. Consequently, followers of Plotinus suffer from metaphysical homesickness. [273]

7. Artists are less than art and art is less than nature. So artists must be less than nature. [283]

8. No velvet paintings of Elvis Presley are works of art. All works of art are lies which rob wholesome qualities from experience. Therefore, no velvet paintings of Elvis Presley are lies which rob wholesome qualities from experience. [293]

9. The deception of art is not real deception. Fear invoked by drama is deception of art. Thus, fear invoked by art is not real deception. [2103]

10. All ugly objects are failures in aesthetic response. No beautiful objects are ugly objects. So all beautiful objects are successes in aesthetic response. [2113]

V. RULES OF THE SYLLOGISM

A. EXPLANATION OF THE FIVE RULES OF THE SYLLOGISM

To be valid any syllogism must satisfy the first FOUR RULES we shall discuss next. In addition, there is a FIFTH RULE which syllogisms must satisfy in order to be valid from the HYPOTHETICAL viewpoint. If a syllogism violates one or more of these rules, then it is invalid. Since there are **256** syllogistic forms, and since each form has its own corresponding Venn diagram, these rules offer a more efficient test for validity.

B. THE FIVE RULES

RULE 1. THE MIDDLE TERM MUST BE DISTRIBUTED AT LEAST ONCE. A syllogism which violates this rule commits the FALLACY OF UNDISTRIBUTED MIDDLE.

EXAMPLE

Decide whether the following syllogism satisfies Rule 1.

Some opinions are revolutionary opinions.
Some opinions are conservative opinions.
So some conservative opinions are revolutionary opinions.

ANALYSIS

The middle term is "opinions." Since it appears in I sentences and since NO terms are distributed in I sentences, the middle term is undistributed.

So this syllogism violates Rule 1 by comitting the fallacy of UNDISTRIBUTED MIDDLE.

QUIZ 16

For each syllogism below decide whether it satisfies Rule 1.

1   All revolutionary opinions are opinions.
All conservative opinions are opinions.
So all conservative opinions are revolutionary opinions. [2123]
2.   All revolutionary opinions are opinions.
Some conservative opinions are not revolutionary opinions.
So some conservative opinions are not opinions. [2133]

RULE 2. IF A TERM IS DISTRIBUTED IN THE CONCLUSION THEN IT MUST ALSO BE DISTRIBUTED IN THE PREMISE. A syllogism which violates this rule commits the FALLACY OF ILLICIT PROCESS.

When the major term is distributed in the conclusion [E and O sentences], but not in the major premise, then the syllogism commits the fallacy of ILLICIT PROCESS OF THE MAJOR.

When the minor term is distributed in the conclusion [A and E sentences], but not in the minor premise, then the syllogism commits the fallacy of ILLICIT PROCESS OF THE MINOR.

EXAMPLE

Decide whether the following syllogism violates Rule 2.

All sanguine lyrics are romantic lyrics.
All romantic lyrics are love-lyrics
So all love-lyrics are sanguine lyrics.

ANALYSIS

The conclusion is an A sentence. In A sentences the subject (minor) term is distributed, so "love-lyrics" is distributed in the conclusion.

But "love-lyrics" is not distributed in the minor premise, since it serves as the predicate of an **A** sentence.

So this syllogism violates Rule 2 by committing the Fallacy of ILLICIT PROCESS OF THE MINOR.

QUIZ 17

For each syllogism below decide whether it violates Rule 2.

1. Some romantic lyrics are not sanguine lyrics.
    Some love-lyrics are romantic lyrics.
    Some love-lyrics are not sanguine lyrics. [202]

2. All romantic lyrics are sanguine lyrics.
    No love-lyrics are romantic lyrics.
    So no love-lyrics are sanguine lyrics. [212]

RULE 3. A SYLLOGISM CANNOT HAVE TWO NEGATIVE PREMISES.

EXAMPLE

Decide whether the following syllogism violates Rule 3.

Some musical modes are not Phrygian modes.
Some musical modes are not Dorian modes.
So some Dorian modes are not phrygian modes.

ANALYSIS

The major premise and the minor premise are both **O** sentences. **O** sentences are negative. Thus, this syllogism violates Rule 2.

QUIZ 18

For each syllogism below decide whether it violates Rule 3.

1. All Phrygian modes are nonDorian modes.
    Some nonDorian modes are not musical modes.
    So some musical modes are not Phrygian modes. [222]

2. No Phrygian modes are Dorian modes.
    Some Dorian modes are not nonmusical modes. [232]
    So some nonmusical modes are not Phrygian modes.

RULE 4. IF A SYLLOGISM HAS A NEGATIVE PREMISE, THEN IT MUST HAVE A NEGATIVE CONCLUSION. AND IF A SYLLOGISM HAS A NEGATIVE CONCLUSION, THEN IT MUST HAVE EXACTLY ONE NEGATIVE PREMISE.

EXAMPLE

Decide whether the following syllogism violates Rule 4.

No cosmetic arts are performing arts.
Some therapeutic arts are cosmetic arts
So some therapeutic arts are performing arts.

ANALYSIS

The major premise, an **E** sentence, is negative. The conclusion, an **I** sentence, is affirmative. Thus, this syllogism violates Rule 4.

For each syllogism below decide whether it violates Rule 4.

1. Some cosmetic arts are therapeutic arts.
   Some therapeutic arts are performing arts.
   So some performing arts are cosmetic arts. [242]
2. Some cosmetic arts are therapeutic arts.
   Some therapeutic arts are performing arts.
   So some performing arts are not cosmetic arts. [252]

RULE 5. A SYLLOGISM CANNOT HAVE TWO UNIVERSAL PREMISES AND A PARTICULAR CONCLUSION. This rule applies only to syllogisms that are being considered from the hypothetical viewpoint. If we are considering a syllogism from an existential viewpoint, we use only the first four rules.

EXAMPLE

Decide whether the following syllogism violates Rule 5.

> No flesh tones are half-tones.
> No half-tones are earth tones.
> So some earth tones are not flesh tones.

ANALYSIS

Both premises are E sentences. E sentences are universal. The conclusion is an O sentence, so it is particular.

The syllogism violates Rule 5, so it cannot be valid from the hypothetical viewpoint.

For each syllogism below decide whether it violates Rule 5.

1. All flesh tones are earth tones.
   Some half-tones are not earth tones.
   So no half-tones are flesh tones. [262]
2. No half-tones are flesh tones.
   All earth tones are half-tones.
   So all earth tones are flesh tones. [272]

EXERCISE #5

A. Test the following syllogisms for validity using both Venn diagrams and the five rules for the syllogism. If you find any syllogism that is valid from an existential viewpoint but is invalid from the hypothetical viewpoint, just explain that this is the case.

1. Some exhibitionists are exhilarationists.
   Some exhilarationists are hedonists.
   So some hedonists are exhibitionists. [282]
2. Some poets are seers.
   Some artists are not seers.
   So some artists are not poets. [292]
3. Some dramatic advances are not technical advances.
   Some dramatic advances are not poetic advances.
   So no poetic advances are technical advances. [2102]

4. All acts of imitation are second-rate acts.
   No acts of imitation are good acts.
   So no good acts are second-rate acts. [2112]
5. No acts of genius are craft activities.
   Some acts of genius are acts productive of craft.
   So some acts productive of craft are not craft activities. [2122]
6. No statments by Winckelman are statements supported in *Laocoon*.
   All statements supported in *Laocoon* are statements made by Lessing.
   So some statements made by Lessing are not statements by Winckelman. [2132]
7. Some pretty poems are not beautiful poems.
   Some Shakespearean sonnets are beautiful poems.
   So some Shakespearean sonnets are pretty poems. [201]
8. All senses are carriers of divine truth.
   Some carriers of divine truth are aesthetic symbols.
   So some aesthetic symbols are senses. [211]
9. All horrible paintings are hideous paintings.
   No Renaissance paintings are hideous paintings.
   So no Renaissance paintings are horrible paintings. [221]
10. All thoughts are feelings shaped into ideas.
    No feelings shaped into ideas are works of art.
    So no works of art are thoughts. [231]

B. For each item below decide whether it is a syllogism. If it is, decide whether it is valid using the Five Rules for Syllogism. Note: as above, the argument might be a standard-form syllogism if the sentences are restated in different order.

1. Since all moments of play are moments of illusion, and since some moments of art are moments of illusion, it must be the case that some moments of art are moments of illusion. [241]
2. Spectators' enjoyment of fighting games is parallel to enjoyment of tragedy. Enjoyment of tragedy is parallel to aesthetic experiences. So aesthetic experiences must be parallel to spectators' enjoyment of fighting games. [251]
3. All things that are true of works of art are things that are true of natural objects. No perceptions of beauty are things that are true of natural objects. Thus, some perceptions of beauty are things that are true of works of art. [261]
4. No beautiful things are unseen things and, since all heard things are unseen things, it follows that no heard things are beautiful things. [271]
5. All disinterested pleasures are aesthetic pleasures, because some pleasures with a purpose are not aesthetic pleasures and no disinterested pleasures are pleasures with a purpose. [281]
6. Since some expressions of emotion are transmissions of feeling, it follows that some theatrical works are translations of feeling since some theatrical works are expressions of emotion. [291]
7. All ungraceful emotional manifestations are inharmonious manifestations, and some unrythmic manifestations are ungraceful emotional manifestations. This leads us to conlcude that some rhythmic manifestations are inharmonious manifestations. [2101]
8. Some generalities are necessities and some rules of craft are necessities. Thus, some rules of craft are generalities. [2111]
9. Heterogeneous objects are not homogeneous objects. And multifaceted objects are not homogeneous objects. So all multifaceted objects are heterogeneous objects. [2121]

10. No nineteenth-century artistic processes are pure processes. All processes of abstraction are pure processes. Some nineteenth-century processes are not processes of abstraction. [2131]

VI. TRANSLATING INTO STANDARD FORM

A. EXPLANATION

We cannot test a syllogism for validity using Venn Diagrams or the Rules for Syllogism, unless the syllogism is in STANDARD FORM. In ordinary language we often find arguments which are NOT in standard form, but which could be TRANSLATED into standard form.

There are TWO ways that an argument can fail to be in standard form.
> 1. One or more of its sentences may not be in standard categorical form.
> 2. It may not contain three terms, as it stands.

So we need to consider two problems. How might we translate a SENTENCE into standard CATEGORICAL form? And how might we translate an ARGUMENT into proper SYLLOGISTIC form?

B. TRANSLATING SENTENCES INTO STANDARD CATEGORICAL FORM

ANY sentence can be translated into an EQUIVALENT standard-form categorical sentence. When we do these translations we must be sure that the new sentence has the same meaning as the original sentence. Barker suggests TEN kinds of problems requiring such translating.

1. PREDICATE AS ADJECTIVE. Where the predicate is an adjective rather than a noun, we may decide WHAT the adjective is DESCRIBING and add it to the sentence.

EXAMPLE

Translate this sentence into standard form.
All shades of purple are vibrant.

ANALYSIS

The predicate, "**vibrant,**" is an adjective which describes shades of purple. So we may translate the sentence like this:
All shades of purple are vibrant shades.

2. VERB OTHER THAN "ARE." Where the main verb in a sentence is not "are" we can move the verb into the predicate.

EXAMPLE

Translate this sentence into standard form.
All lithographers claim to have artistic talent.

ANALYSIS

The verb we wish to move is "**claim.**" A proper translation of this sentence into standard form is
All lithographers are people who claim to have artistic talent.

3. "TO BE" IN PAST OR FUTURE TENSE. The copula of a standard-form categorical sentence should always be "are" or "are not." Where the copula is in the past or present tense we can move that verb into the predicate.

EXAMPLE

Translate this sentence into standard form.
Some disciples of Croce were disciples of Vico.

ANALYSIS

The verb to change is "**were.**" A proper translation of this sentence is
Some disciples of Croce are people who are disciples of Vico.

4. NON-STANDARD WORD ORDER. We may simply have to REARRANGE a sentence's word order to put it into standard form.

EXAMPLE

Translate this sentence into standard form.
Potters are all skilled glazers.

ANALYSIS

This sentence is universal and affirmative, so our best bet is to translate this into an **A** sentence. The subject is "**potters**" and the predicate is "**glazers.**" So a proper translation of this sentence is
All potters are skilled glazers.

5. SINGULAR SENTENCES. Where the subject or predicate TERM is a SINGULAR term, we can translate the sentence into categorical form by making the subject the CLASS of things which are IDENTICAL to that term.

EXAMPLE

Translate this sentence into standard form.
Dali is a surrealist.

ANALYSIS

The sentence is affirmative. The subject is "**Dali**" and the predicate is "**surrealist.**" A proper translation of this sentence is
All people who are identical to Dali are surrealists.

6. NO SPECIFIC INDICATION OF QUANTITY. Often, when a sentence contains no indication of quantity, we can still decide whether the sentence is UNIVERSAL or PARTICULAR. This decision allows us to determine which quantifier should be added in our translation of the sentence.

EXAMPLE 1

Translate this sentence into standard form.
A photograph by Arbus hangs in the Walker art gallery.

ANALYSIS

This sentence is saying something about a *particular* photograph. A proper translation of this sentence into standard form is
Some photographs by Arbus are photographs which hang in the Walker art gallery.

EXAMPLE 2

Translate this sentence into standard form.

A photograph is an image recorded by a camera.

ANALYSIS

This sentence is saying something which applies to *all* photographs, so it should be translated as a *universal* sentence. A proper translation of this sentence into standard form is

All photographs are images recorded by a camera.

7. "NOT" APPEARING IN THE MIDDLE OF A UNIVERSAL SENTENCE. When the word "not" appears in a universal sentence we have to ask whether it belongs to the copula or to the predicate. Our decision should be based on what the speaker probably intends to mean. Is the speaker talking about *all* members of the subject class? If so, then the sentence should be *universal*, if not then it should be *particular*. Is the speaker *affirming* something about the subject? If so, then the sentence should be *affirmative*, if not, then the sentence should be *negative*.

EXAMPLE

Translate this sentence into standard categorical form.

All photographers are not users of Nikons.

ANALYSIS

This sentence is *denying* something, so the sentence should be translated as a *negative* sentence. This sentence is not saying something about every photographer, it is only saying that *some* photographers use cameras other than Nikons. So a proper translation of this sentence is

Some photographers are not users of Nikons.

8. "ONLY" AND "NONE BUT." In general, "ONLY" and "NONE BUT" can be translated as "ALL," if the SUBJECT and PREDICATE are switiched.

EXAMPLE

Translate the following sentence into standard categorical form.

Only geniuses are virtuosos.

ANALYSIS

We may translate "ONLY" as "ALL." If we also **switch** the **subject** and **predicate**, then a proper translation of this sentence into standard form is

All virtuosos are geniuses.

9. "ONLY SOME" AND "ALL EXCEPT." A sentence which uses a phrase like "only some" or "all except" must be carefully translated, in order to avoid any ambiguities. "ONLY SOME S ARE P," usually means "SOME S ARE P and SOME S ARE NOT P." "ALL EXCEPT S ARE P," usually means "ALL NON-S ARE P," and may also mean "NO S ARE P."

EXAMPLE

Translate this sentence into standard categorical form.

Only some of Picasso's paintings were done during his Blue Period.

ANALYSIS

"ONLY SOME S ARE P" usally means "SOME S ARE P and SOME S ARE NOT P." So a proper translation of this sentence into standard form is

Some of Picasso's paintings are from his Blue Period and some of Picasso's paintings are not from his Blue Period.

10. IMPLIED TERMS. Sometimes a term is implied, but not stated. Where this happens, we often have to introduce a new term. For instance, is the sentence about a specific place, even though "place" is not mentioned? If so, the translation can make use of "place."

EXAMPLE

Translate this sentence into standard categorical form.

When Mistral paints he must have silence.

ANALYSIS

This sentence implicitly refers to **all** the times that Mistral paints. A proper translation of this sentence into standard form is

All times when Mistral paints are times when Mistral must have silence.

QUIZ 21

Translate the following sentences into standard categorical form.

1. Classical composers were particular about the sonata form. [2140]
2. Musicians visited our school yesterday. [2150]

C. PUTTING ARGUMENTS INTO SYLLOGISTIC FORM.

In addition to putting sentences into standard categorical form, we may have to REDUCE THE NUMBER OF TERMS in an argument, in order to make the argument a standard-form categorical syllogism.

In general, where (1) an argument contains two premises and a conclusion, each of which is a categorical sentence and (2) the number of terms may be reduced by replacing a sentence with another sentence which is logically equivalent, we may use operations such as Obversion and Contraposition, where appropriate, to reduce the number of terms.

EXAMPLE

Translate this argument into standard form. And decide whether it is valid.

All acrylics are paints. All nonacrylics are nonpolymers. So all polymers are paints.

ANALYSIS

If we **contrapose** the **second** premise we get "All polymers are acrylics." This reduces the number of terms in the argument to three: **acrylics, paints,** and **polymers.** The argument may now be put in standard syllogistic form.

All acrylics are paints.
All polymers are acrylics.
So all polymers are paints.

This is an **AAA-1** syllogism, so it is valid

37

For each argument below, decide whether it can be translated into standard syllogistic form. If it can, translate it, and decide whether it is valid.

1. Some concertos are piano concertos, but no violin concertos are nonconcertos, so no violin concertos are piano concertos. [2160]

2. No nontubas are nonwoodwinds. No woodwinds are trombones. So some trombones are not tubas. [2151]

EXERCISE #6

A. Translate each sentence into a logically equivalent, standard-form categorical sentence.

1. Languages are symbol systems. [2161]
2. Pictures are symbolic. [2142
3. Art is imitation. [2152]
4. Photographs resemble their objects. [2162]
5. Fake works of art are all forgeries. [2143]
6. No x-ray photographs are not photographs. [2153]
7. None but the perceptive deserve Public Television. [2163]
8. No films are worth seeing. [2144]
9. Whenever Maria sings, the windows rattle. [2154]
10. A single quantum of light may excite a retinal receptor. [2141]

B. For each argument below, decide whether it can be translated into standard syllogistic form. If it can, translate it, and decide whether it is valid.

1. Some productions are nonperformances. Some performances are not comedies. So some comedies are not productions. [2145]

2. All choreographed works are dances. All nondances are nonwaltzes. So all waltzes are choreographed works. [2159]

3. All nonpuzzles are nonperplexities. No nonperplexities are nonquandries. So all quandries are puzzles.

4. Some mirrors are nonmedia. Some nonmedia are not languages. So some languages are not mirrors. [2155]

5. Expressive portrayals are descriptive portrayals. Documentaries are descriptive portrayals. So documentaries are expressive portrayals. [2146]

6. Sculpture honors material in two ways. Some nonpaintings honor material in two ways. So some paintings are sculptures. [2158]

7. A song's assets reduce its liabilities. Harmony is a song's asset. So harmony reduces a song's liabilities. [2148]

8. A diagram is a map. A map is a model. So a diagram is a model. [2157]

9. Schemata are all metaphors. Some scores are not nonschemata. So some scores are metaphors. [2147]

10. All films except Bergman's have played at the Bijou. *Amarcord* is at the Bijou. So *Amarcord* is not a Bergman film. [2156]

CHAPTER 3 - THE LOGIC OF TRUTH FUNCTIONS

I. ARGUMENTS CONTAINING COMPOUND SENTENCES

A COMPOUND SENTENCE is any SENTENCE containing one or more SHORTER SENTENCES as part of itself. For example, "Lewis Carroll is an author and Charles Dodgson is an Oxford Don," is a compound sentence. It contains TWO short SENTENCES ("Lewis Carroll is an author," "Charles Dodgson is an Oxford Don") connected by the word "and."

Sentences can be combined to form compound sentences through the use of logical connectives such as NEGATION, DISJUNCTION, CONJUNCTION, and CONDITIONALS. Arguments consisting of sentences made up of these kinds of logical relations are ARGUMENTS CONTAINING COMPOUND SENTENCES.

A. ELEMEMTARY FORMS OF VALID AND INVALID ARGUMENTS

Barker selects the following samples of valid and invalid arguments (where p,q, and r stand for entire sentences). With these forms of valid and invalid arguments, we can determine whether particular arguments are valid or invalid by determining whether those arguments have the same form as one of the arguments on the list.

1. NEGATION (Any "not" sentence)

Double	$\dfrac{\text{Not (not p)}}{\therefore p}$	$\dfrac{p}{\therefore \text{not (not p)}}$
negation:		

Here we let the letters "p," "q," "r," etc. mark the places where simple sentences are located. Once this is correctly done, the identification will be easy.

EXAMPLE

Lewis Caroll is Charles Dodgson.
Therefore it is not the case that Lewis Carroll is not Charles Dodgson.

ANAYLSIS

Let p = "Lewis Carroll is Charles Dodgson."

We can begin by replacing the premise with p:

$\underline{p}$
Therefore it is NOT the case that Lewis Carroll is NOT Charles Dodgson

Notice that the conclusion contains two negations. The second occurrence denies that Lewis Carroll is Charles Dodgson -- it is saying "not p." Replace that to get the following:

$\underline{p}$
Therefore it is NOT the case that (not p)

Now reduce "it is not the case" simply to "not."

$\underline{p}$
Therefore not (not p)

Use three dots ($\therefore$) to stand for the word "therefore." The argument now reads,

$\underline{p}$
$\therefore$ not (not p)

Thus this argument has exactly the form of DOUBLE NEGATION, and it is therefore VALID. We can follow this procedure in each of the upcoming argument forms.

2. DISJUNCTION (Any "or" sentence)

Disjunctive	p or q	p or q
argument:	$\dfrac{\text{Not p}}{\therefore q}$	$\dfrac{\text{Not q}}{\therefore p}$
Invalid	p or q	p or q
disjunctive	$\underline{p}$	$\underline{q}$
argument:	$\therefore$ not q	$\therefore$ not p

Often we encounter an argument that is valid but does not precisely match the forms we have been given. One way of dealing with a situation like this is to TRANSLATE the given argument INTO one of the STANDARD FORMS. This may be done in either of two ways: (1) replace a premise or conclusion by something logically equivalent to it (this will be seen in an upcoming discussion of logical equivalence) or (2) REARRANGE the ORDER OF THE PREMISES so that they correspond to the standard forms.

EXAMPLE

Charles Dodgson does not remain obscure.
Either Charles Dodgson remains obscure or he meets Alice Liddell.
Therefore Charles Dodgson meets Alice Liddell.

Rearranging the premises, we now have the form of a VALID DISJUNCTIVE argument:

> Either Charles Dodgson remains obscure or he meets Alice Liddell.
> Charles Dodgson does not remain obscure.
> Therefore Charles Dodgson meets Alice Liddell.
> The argument now reads,
>
> p or q
> Not p
> ∴ q

QUIZ 1

Take the following arguments and identify their general argument forms (rearranging into standard form if necessary). Then state whether the arguments are valid or invalid.

1. It is not the case that Alice does not go through the Looking Glass.
   Therefore Alice goes through the Looking Glass. [3158]

2. Alice meets the Red Queen.
   Either Alice meets the Red Queen or Alice loses her way.
   Alice does not lose her way. [3161]

3. CONJUNCTION (Any "and" sentence)

Conjunctive arguments:	Not (p and q) p ∴ not q	Not (p and q) q ∴ not p	p and q ∴ p
Invalid conjunctive arguments:	Not (p and q) Not p ∴ q	Not (p and q) Not q \p	

QUIZ 2

Take the following arguments and identify their general argument forms (rearranging into standard form if necessary). Then state whether the arguments are valid or invalid.

1. Tweedledee and Tweedledum are fond of poetry.
   Therefore Tweedledee is fond of poetry. [3162]

2. It is not the case that the Walrus and the Carpenter go hungry.
   The Walrus does not go hungry.
   Therefore the Carpenter goes hungry. [3159]

4. CONDITIONALS (Any "if-then" sentence)

The first part of a conditional sentence (that part contained in the "if" clause) is called the ANTECEDENT. The second part of a conditional sentence (that part contained in the "then" clause) is called the CONSEQUENT.

Modus ponens	If p then q p ∴ q	*Modus tollens:*	If p then q Not q ∴ not p	Chain argument	If p then q If q then r ∴ if p then r
Reductio ad absurdum	If p then not p ∴ not p		If p then both q and not q ∴ not p		

Invalid Conditionals

Fallacy of affirming the consequent:	If p then q q ∴ p	Fallacy of denying the antecedent:	If p then q Not p ∴ not q

41

Take the following arguments and identify their general argument forms (rearranging into standard form if necessary). Then state whether the arguments are valid or invalid.

1. If Alice meets the White Queen, then Alice advances two squares.
    Alice meets the White Queen.
    Therefore Alice advances two squares. [3160]
2. If the forest shakes, then Humpty Dumpty has fallen off the wall.
    Humpty Dumpty has fallen off the wall.
    Therefore the forest shakes. [3164]

5. DILEMMAS

These arguments combine conditionals and disjunctions in a certain manner, and they sometimes include negation also.

Simple constructive dilemma:	If p then q If r then q p or r ∴ q	Simple destructive dilemma:	If p then q If p then r Not q or not r ∴ not p
Complex constructive dilemma:	If p then q If r then s p or r ∴ q or s	Complex destructive dilemma:	If p then q If r then s Not q or not s ∴ not p or not r

Take the following arguments and identify their general argument forms (rearranging into standard form if necessary). Then state whether the arguments are valid or invalid.

1. If the White Knight appears, then Alice will be a prisoner.
    If the Red Knight appears, then Alice will be a prisoner.
    Either the Red Knight appears or the White Knight appears
    Therefore Alice will be a prisoner. [3165]
2. If the Red Queen is real, then the White Knight is real.
    If the Red Queen is real, then the White Queen is real.
    Either the White Knight is not real or the White Queen is not real.
    Therefore the Red Queen is not real. [3163]

EXERCISE #1

Take the following arguments and identify their general argument forms (rearranging into standard form if necessary). Then state whether the arguments are valid or invalid.

1. If the Cheshire-Cat is normal, then it will stay in the tree.
    The Cheshire-Cat does not stay in the tree.
    Therefore the Cheshire-Cat is not normal. [301]
2. Alice is in a pool of tears and the Mouse is swimming.
    Therefore Alice is in a pool of tears. [312]
3. It is not the case that Alice does not fall down the Rabbit Hole.
    Therefore Alice falls down the Rabbit Hole. [307]
4. The Rabbit sends in Bill the Lizard.
    The Rabbit will not send in both Mary Ann the housemaid and Bill the Lizard.
    Therefore the Rabbit does not send in Mary Ann the housemaid. [309]

5. If there is a Mad Tea-Party, then the Dormouse is asleep.
   The Dormouse is asleep.
   Therefore there is a Mad Tea-Party. [302]

6. Either Alice remains the same size or Alice drinks from the bottle.
   Alice does not remain the same size.
   Therefore Alice drinks from the bottle. [314]

7. Alice and the Blue Caterpillar won't both smoke the hookah.
   Alice won't smoke the hookah.
   Therefore the Blue Caterpillar will smoke the hookah. [310]

8. If the Gryphon asks her, then Alice will dance the Lobster-Quadrille.
   If the Mock Turtle asks her, then Alice will dance the Lobster-Quadrille.
   Either the Gryphon or the Mock Turtle asks her.
   Therefore Alice will dance the Lobster-Quadrille. [304]

9. Alice is ten inches tall.
   Either Alice is ten inches tall or the White Rabbit is in a hurry.
   Therefore the White Rabbit is not in a hurry. [313]

10. There will not be both a Caucus-Race and a long tale.
    There is a Caucus-Race.
    Therefore there will not be a long tale. [308]

11. If the Duchess is in a bad mood, then she will throw the baby at Alice.
    The Duchess is in a bad mood.
    Therefore the Duchess will throw the baby at Alice. [311]

12. It is not the case that Father William is both old and upright.
    Father William is not upright.
    Therefore Father William is old. [317]

13. Either the Knave of Hearts is a witness or the Hatter is a witness.
    If the Knave of Hearts is a witness, then the tarts are stolen.
    If the Hatter is a witness, then the tarts remain on the table.
    Therefore either the tarts are stolen or the tarts remain on the table. [303]

14. If the Queen cuts off their heads, then the Queen doesn't cut off their heads.
    Therefore the Queen doesn't cut off their heads. [319]

15. Either Alice eats the cake or Alice remains in the hallway.
    Alice does not remain in the hallway.
    Therefore Alice eats the cake. [315]

16. If it's a Whiting, then it cleans boots.
    If it's a Whiting, then it cleans shoes.
    Either it will not clean boots or it will not clean shoes.
    Therefore it is not a Whiting. [306]

17. If the Hatter eats what he sees, then the March Hare sees what he eats.
    The Hatter does not eat what he sees.
    Therefore the March Hare does not see what he eats. [318]

18. If the Gryphon laughs, then the Mock Turtle both sobs and doesn't sob.
    Therefore the Gryphon does not laugh. [305]

19. If Alice is ten inches tall, then she will sit quietly.
    If the Knave is guilty, then the Queen is right.
    Either Alice will not sit quietly or the Queen isn't right.
    Therefore either Alice is not ten inches tall or the Knave is not guilty. [320]

20. If Alice will find the Rose Garden, then Alice will be invited to play croquet.
    If Alice leaves the Party, then Alice will find the Rose Garden.
    Therefore if Alice leaves the Party, then Alice will be invited to play croquet. [316]

II. TRUTH FUNCTIONS AND THEIR GROUPINGS

Many compound sentences are such that if you knew the truth or falsity of their parts you could determine the truth or falsity of the entire compound. When this is so, it may be said that the truth or falsity of the compound is a FUNCTION of the truth or falsity of its parts. For example,

> The Braves will win the Eastern Division and the Dodgers
> will win the Western Division.

(1)   This is a compound sentence consisting of two simple sentences: "The Braves will win the Eastern Division" and "The Dodgers will win the Western Division."

(2)   A person making this prediction will be saying something TRUE only if both teams win -- otherwise his prediction will be FALSE.

A. THE LOGICAL CONNECTIVES

Sentences like the above are called TRUTH-FUNCTIONAL SENTENCES. This section states the various ways in which the truth values (the t's and f's) of the components of these sentences may be affected by certain logical connectives (or "logical operators").

We shall discuss FIVE such logical connectives, and each can be represented on a "table." The purpose of a TRUTH TABLE is to SHOW us ALL the POSSIBLE COMBINATIONS of TRUTH and FALSITY that a truth functional sentence can have.

I.   NEGATION: expressed by the word "not."
   Symbol: a dash
   Rule: REVERSES truth values
      (Sample truth table:)

p	-p
t	f
f	t

(If p is true, its negation is false; if p is false, its negation is true.)

II.   CONJUNCTION: expressed by the word "and."
   Symbol: the ampersand (&).
   Rule: TRUE when ALL COMPONENTS are TURE, FALSE OTHERWISE.

   (sample truth table:)

p	q	p&q
t	t	t
f	t	f
t	f	f
f	f	f

III. DISJUNCTION: expressed by the word: "or."
   Symbol: a wedge (v).
   Rule: FALSE only when ALL COMPONENTS are FALSE, TRUE OTHERWISE.

   (sample truth table:)

p	q	pvq
t	t	t
f	t	t
t	f	t
f	f	f

IV.   CONDTIONAL: expressed by the words "if-then."
   Symbol: the horseshoe ($\supset$)
   RULE: FALSE only when the ANTECEDENT is TRUE and the CONSEQUENT is FALSE, TRUE OTHERWISE.

(1)

p	q	p⊃q
t	t	t
f	t	t
t	f	f
f	f	t

(2)

p	q	q⊃p
t	t	t
f	t	f
t	f	t
f	f	t

V. BICONDITIONAL: expressed by the
words "if and only if."
Symbol: three bars ($\equiv$)
Rule: TRUE when BOTH parts have
the SAME TRUTH VALUE, FALSE
if they are MIXED.

(sample truth table:)

p	q	p $\equiv$ q
t	t	t
f	t	f
t	f	f
f	f	t

B. TRANSLATION INTO SYMBOLIC FORM

It is easy to determine the truth or falsity of compound sentences by noting the truth values of their components and looking at the appropriate rows and columns of the truth tables. This process is even easier if the compound sentence is translated into its SYMBOLIC FORM.

To "translate" a compound sentence, we may choose a key letter to stand for a particular sentence. For example, "The Braves will win the Eastern Division and the Dodgers will win the Western Division" can be translated as "B&D" if we let "B" be short for "The Braves will win the Eastern Division" and "D" be short for "The Dodgers will win the Western Division."

Once the sentence is abreviated, we can apply the rule for conjunction to any truth values that might be attached to the letters B and D. That is, if B is *true* but D is *false*, then the compound "B&D" is FALSE. But if B is *true and D is true*, then the compound "B&D" is TRUE. (To see this, look at the truth table that shows a conjunction for any two sentences.)

EXAMPLE

Translate the following into its symbolic form. In doing so, let "O" be short for "The Baltimore Orioles will win the World Series" and "T" be short for "The Detroit Tigers will win the World Series."

Either the Baltimore Orioles will win the World Series or the Detroit Tigers will win the World Series.

ANALYSIS

Since this is a DISJUNCTION between two simple sentences ("O" and "T"), it can be written as "Either O or T." And since the symbol for disjunction is a wedge (v), the compound sentence can be more briefly symbolized as "OvT."

EXAMPLE

Assume that it is true that the Orioles do win the World series and that it is false that the Tigers won. What would be the truth value of the compound sentence "OvT"?

ANALYSIS

The rule for disjunction states that a disjunction is false only if both components are false, and it is true otherwise. In this case, if we assign the value of *true* to "O" and the value of *false* to "T," then the truth value of the compound sentence "OvT" would be TRUE.

EXAMPLE

Now assume that neither team won the World Series. What would be the truth value of the compound sentence?

ANALYSIS

The rule for disjunction states that a disjunction is false only if all components are false; it is true otherwise. In this case, if we assign the value of *false* to "O" and the value of *false* to "T," then the truth value of the compound sentence "OvT" would be FALSE.

QUIZ 5

Let "W" be short for "The Chicago White Sox win the playoffs" and let "Y" be short for "The New York Yankees win the playoffs." Assume that "W" is true and "Y" is false.

First, translate the following compound sentences into their symbolic form. Second, determine their truth or falsity.

1. If the Chicago White Sox win the playoffs then the New York Yankees win the playoffs. [322]
2. The New York Yankees win the playoffs if and only if the Chicago White Sox win the playoffs. [321]

C. LOGICAL PUNCTUATION

In many cases compound sentences require LOGICAL PUNCTUATION when translated into symbolic form. The reason for this is the same as the reason why PARENTHESES are used in math: to AVOID AMBIGUITY. Without any rules to guide us, the expression $5 + 3 \times 2 = ?$ can mean either 16 [as in $(5 + 3) \times 2$] or 11 [as in $5 + (3 \times 2)$]. This same problem of ambiguity can be found in translating certain compound sentences.

For example, without proper punctuation, the following sentence is ambiguous: "The Cleveland Indians activated Steve Farr and the Seattle Mariners recalled Orlando Mercado or the Minnesota Twins placed Al Williams on the disabled list." This sentence can mean

(1) (Steve Farr was activated and Orlando Mercado was recalled) OR (Al Williams was placed on the disabled list)

or

(2) (Steve Farr was activated) AND (either Orlando Mercado was recalled or Al Williams was placed on the disabled list).

On the first interpretation, the sentence is a *disjunction* with a conjunction in its opening part. On the second interpretation, the sentence is a *conjunction* with a disjunction in its last part. The use of parentheses removes the ambiguity, and tells the reader which interpretation is intended (and this makes a difference to Al Williams!).

It is for reasons such as these that it becomes important to GROUP the components of truth functional compound sentences in a correct manner. And the way to do this is to use parentheses (and, if needed, brackets) to mark out the intended meaning of the sentence.

NOTE: In only one case does Barker assume a rule that allows us skip the use of parentheses. This is with negation, and the rule states that WHATEVER IMMEDIATELY FOLLOWS A NEGATION SIGN WILL BE NEGATED. Thus, -p⊃q will be interpreted as a conditional with a negated antecedent. But -(p⊃q) will be interpreted as the negation of an entire conditional. In the first instance the "p" is being negated, in the second instance the "p⊃q" is being negated.

EXAMPLE

Symbolize the following sentence. Use punctuation where appropriate.

Either Detroit will not win the Eastern Division or both Baltimore and California will play in the World Series. (Let "D" be short for "Detroit will win the Eastern Division," let "B" be short for "Baltimore will play in the World Series," and let "C" be short for "California will play in the World Series.")

ANALYSIS

First, notice what logical operators are used in the sentence. Here there is a disjunction, a negation, and a conjunction.

Second, determine which is the major operator i.e., ask yourself what is mainly being said in the sentence. Here it is an EITHER...OR...(viz., Either Detroit...or both Baltimore...).

Finally, work your way into the parts of the major operator. (1) Look at the first part of the disjunction -- it's a negation:"-D." (2) Notice the second part -- it's a conjunction:"B&C." (3) Now if you join both parts with the disjunction, and be sure to separate the conjunction with parentheses (you don't need to do this with the negated "D"), then you get "-Dv(B&C)."

QUIZ 6

Symbolize the following.

1. If the Giants don't win the Western Division, then the Dodgers will. (Let "G" be short for "The Giants win the Western Division" and let "D" be short for "The Dodgers will win the Western Division.") [324]

2. It is not the case that both Gwynn from San Diego and Francona from Montreal are leading the League in batting. (Let "G" be short for "Gwynn from San Diego is leading the League in batting" and let "F" be short for "Francona from Montreal is leading the League in batting.") [323]

* * *

Before doing the upcoming exercises, some HINTS on translation might be helpful. The following are examples of variations in ordinary language which conform to the rules for the logical relations:

(1) NEGATION can be expressed by "not," "it is not the case that," "doesn't," "won't," and "will fail to."

(2) CONJUNCTION can be expressed by "and," "both," "but," "nevertheless," and "although."

(3) DISJUNCTION can be expressed by "or," "either...or...," and "unless."

(4) CONDITIONAL can be expressed by "if p then q," "if p , q," "p provided q," and "p only if q." (Caution should be used if you have an expression of the form "p if q." This is not to be read as equivalent to "if p then q," rather it is to be read as "if q then p.")

(5) BICONDITIONAL can be expressed by "... if and only if..." and "...is a necessary and sufficient condition of..."

47

EXERCISE #2

A. Let "A" be short for "Atlanta wins its conference championship", let "I" be short for "Indianapolis wins its conference championship," let "W" be short for "Washington wins the Superbowl," and let "D" be short for "Dallas wins the Superbowl." Assume that "A" is false, "I" is false, "W" is true, and "D" is false.

First, using the letters given above, abbreviate the following compound sentences. Second, assuming the truth values given above, determine whether the following compound sentences are true or false.

1. Either Atlanta wins its conference championship or Washington will not win the Superbowl. [327]
2. Either Atlanta wins its conference championship and Indianapolis wins its conference championship or Washington wins the Superbowl. [330]
3. Atlanta wins its conference championship and either Indianapolis wins its conference championship or Dallas does not win the Superbowl. [333]
4. Either Atlanta will win its conference championship or Indianapolis will win its conference championship, but it is not the case that both Washington and Dallas will win the Superbowl. [328]
5. Washington will not win the Superbowl unless Atlanta wins its conference championship. [335]
6. Either Washington or Dallas will fail to win the Superbowl. [332]
7. Either Washington or Dallas will win the Superbowl unless both Atlanta and Indianapolis win their conference championships. [336]
8. It is not the case that Washington wins the Superbowl unless Indianapolis does not win its conference championship. [329]
9. Either Washington will win the Superbowl and Dallas will not win the Superbowl or both Atlanta and Indianapolis will win their conference championships. [334]
10. Either it is not the case that both Atlanta and Indianapolis win their conference championships or Washington wins the Superbowl and Dallas does not win the Superbowl. [331]

B. Let "A" be short for "Amherst wins its first game," let "C" be short for "Colgate wins its first game," and let "D" be short for "Dartmouth wins its first game." Assume that A is true, C is false, and D is false.

First, using the letters given above, abbreviate the following compound sentences. Second, assuming the truth values given above, determine whether the following compound sentences are true or false.

1. If Amherst wins its first game, then Colgate wins its first game. [337]
2. Both Amherst and Colgate win their first games only if Dartmouth does not win its first game. [341]
3. Amherst wins its first game if either Colgate wins its first game or Dartmouth wins its first game. [343)
4. Colgate wins its first game if and only if Dartmouth does not win its first game. [339]
5. If Amherst wins its first game then both Colgate and Dartmouth win their first games. [346]
6. Amherst wins its first game if and only if it is not the case that either Colgate or Dartmouth wins its first game. [345]
7. If Amherst wins its first game then either Colgate does not win its first game or Dartmouth does not win its first game. [342]

8. If it is not the case that both Amherst and Colgate win their first games then either Amherst does not win its first game or Colgate does not win its first game. [338]
9. Either Amherst wins its first game and Colgate does not win its first game or if Colgate does not win its first game then Dartmouth does not win its first game. [344]
10. If Dartmouth does not win its first game, then if Colgate does not win its first game, then Amherst wins its first game. [340]

III. TRUTH TABLES

In this section we will use the rules for the logical operators to CONSTRUCT truth tables for compound sentences. Once constructed, we will be in a position to see the various APPLICATIONS of truth tables. Specifically, we will use truth tables to determine (1) IMPLICATION and VALIDITY, (2) EQUIVALENCE, and (3) TAUTOLOGY and CONTRADICTION.

The construction of truth tables rests on the rules for the logical operators.

SUMMARY OF THE RULES

(1) NEGATION: Reverses truth values.
(2) CONJUNCTION: True when all parts are true, false otherwise.
(3) DISJUNCTION: False only when all parts are false, true otherwise.
(4) CONDITIONAL: False only when the antecedent is true and the consequent is false, true in every other case.
(5) BICONDITIONAL: True when both parts are the same, false if they are different.

Truth tables show us all the true/false possibilities that a truth functional sentence can have. A single sentence ("p") can have two possibilities, two sentences ("p," "q") can have four possibilities, three sentences ("p," "q," "r") eight possibilties, and so forth, doubling the number of rows for each additional sentence.

Barker adopts the following STANDARD to be used in SETTING UP a truth table for a certain number of sentences:

p	p	q	p	q	r
t	t	t	t	t	t
f	f	t	f	t	t
	t	f	t	f	t
	f	f	f	f	t
			t	t	f
			f	t	f
			t	f	f
			f	f	f

A. BUILDING TRUTH TABLES

To construct a truth table for a given compound sentence, the following procedure is helpful. FIRST, note the number of different letters and set up the truth table for that number of letters. SECOND, note the major logical operator and construct "auxiliary columns" for each component surrounding the major operator. Once this is correctly done, the final column will represent all the true/false possibilities of the compound sentence.

Construct a truth table for the following sentence: pv-q.

ANALYSIS

First, notice that there are two different letters (p,q). The truth table should be set up starting in the following way:

p	q
t	t
f	t
t	t
f	f

Second, notice that the given sentence is a disjunction with its first part being a "p" and its second part being a negated "q." In order to figure out the disjunction between a "p" and a "-q," you will have to know what the column for a "-q" will look like. So the thing to do now is to set up an auxiliary column for the "-q" (which is essentially the negation of the "q" column):

p	q	-q
t	t	f
f	t	f
t	f	t
f	f	t

Now you are in a position to figure out the column for the entire disjunction. This is done by applying the rule for disjunction to the columns for "p" and "-q." Constructing the final column row by row, you would get the completed truth table:

p	q	-q	pv-q
t	t	f	t
f	t	f	f
t	f	t	t
f	f	t	t

QUIZ 7

Construct truth tables for the following:(1) -p&q [353], (2) -p⊃q [352], (3) pv-p [354].
****

To construct truth tables for more complicated sentences, you basically follow the same procedure. The important thing is to note carefully the logical punctuation.

EXAMPLE

Construct a truth table for (p&q)v-q.

ANALYSIS

First, note the number of different letters in the compound sentence. Since there are only two different letters (p,q), the truth table will be set up starting with two columns and four rows.

Second, note that this is a disjunction between a conjunction "p&q" and a negated "q." The parentheses mark off the left side of the wedge. A truth table for this sentence would have auxiliary columns for "p&q" and "-q," and the rule for disjunction would be applied to those columns:

		*	*	
p	q	p&q	-q	(p&q)v-q
t	t	t	f	t
f	t	f	f	f
t	f	f	t	t
f	f	f	t	t

EXERCISE #3

Construct truth tables for the following compound sentences.

(1) pv(p&q) [355]   (5) (p&q)⊃q [359]   (9) p ≡ (-q⊃-p) [363]
(2) pv(-p&q) [360]   (6) -(p&q)v(p⊃q) [358]   (10) (q⊃p)⊃(p⊃q) [357]
(3) -pv(-p&-q) [362]   (7) (-pvq)⊃r [356]
(4) p⊃(-pv-q) [364]   (8) p⊃(q⊃r) [361]

Once the skill of constructing truth tables has been mastered, the next stage is to use truth tables to tell us certain things about compound sentences and arguments made up of compound sentences (as well as some things about the logic of computers!).

B. TRUTH TABLE TEST FOR IMPLICATION

The first APPLICATION of truth tables involves the use of truth tables to determine LOGICAL IMPLICATION.

IMPLICATION is the relation that holds between one sentence (or a group of sentences) and another. If the first is true, the second necessarily has to be true too.

To determine logical implication, set up a truth table that includes columns for both the sentence(s) supposed doing the implying and the sentence supposedly implied. See whether there is a row in which the first sentence is true and the second sentence is false. If this is so, the implication does not hold. If there is no such row, the implication holds.

EXAMPLE

Does "-(pvq)" imply "-p&-q"?

ANALYSIS

Set up a truth table for both sentences

			*			*
p	q	pvq	-(pvq)	-p	-q	-p&-q
t	t	t	f	f	f	f
f	t	t	f	t	f	f
t	f	t	f	f	t	f
f	f	f	t	t	t	t

Note that there is no row in which the entry for "-(pvq)" is true but the entry for "-p&-q" is false. The truth table shows us that "-(pvq)" does imply "-p&-q."

51

			*		*	
p	q	pvq	-(pvq)	-p	-q	-p&-q
t	t	t	f	f	f	f
f	t	t	f	t	f	f
t	f	t	f	f	t	f
f	f	f	t	t	t	t

QUIZ 8

1. Does "-(p&q)" imply "-pv-q"? [366]
2. Does "-p&-q" imply "-(p&q)"? [372]

C. TRUTH TABLE TEST FOR VALIDITY AND INVALIDITY

The idea of logical implication lies behind the VALIDITY of truth functional arguments, for we can view the premises of an argument as a set of sentences that, taken together, should logically imply the conclusion.

The truth table test for validity utilizes this notion of implication by providing a way in which we can see whether there is any row in which all the premises are true and the conclusion is false. If there is even one such row, then the argument will be INVALID. But if there is no row where the premises are true and the conclusion is false, then the argument will be shown to be VALID.

EXAMPLE

Use a truth table to determine whether the following argument is valid or invalid.

$$p \supset q$$
$$\underline{-p}$$
$$\therefore -q$$

ANALYSIS

There are three steps involved in the truth table test for the validity of an argument.

First, SET UP THE TRUTH TABLE for the number of different letters in the argument.

p	q
t	t
f	t
t	f
f	f

Second, EXPRESS THE ENTIRE ARGUMENT ON THE TRUTH TABLE. That is, draw up a column for each premise and a column for the conclusion.

		1	2	C
p	q	p⊃q	-p	-q
t	t	t	f	f
f	t	t	t	f
t	f	f	f	t
f	f	t	t	t

52

Third, reading row by row, and going from premise(s) to conclusion, LOOK FOR A SINGLE ROW IN WHICH ALL THE PREMISES ARE TRUE AND YET THE CONCLUSION IS FALSE. If you find such a row, then the argumnet is invalid; if you don't, then the argument is valid.

		1	2	C
p	q	p⊃q	-p	-q
t	t	t	f	f
f	t	t	t	f	←
t	f	f	f	t
f	f	t	t	t

The truth table shows that this is an invalid argument. (This table, in fact, demonstrates the fallacy of denying the antecedent.)

QUIZ 9

Use truth tables to determine whether the following arguments are valid or invalid.

1. p⊃q
    r⊃q
    pvr
    ∴ q [365]

2. -(p&q)
    -p
    ∴ q [369]

D. TRUTH TABLE TEST FOR EQUIVALENCE

The next major application of truth tables involves TRUTH-FUNCTIONAL EQUIVALENCE.

Two sentences are truth-functionally equivalent if they are necessarily the SAME as regards their truth and falsity. A truth table can show this by exhibiting all the possible combinations that a compound sentence can have. If the columns for each of the two sentences are exactly alike in EVERY CASE, then the sentences have been shown to be equivalent. If there is even a single row in which they differ, then the sentences are not equivalent.

EXAMPLE

Use a truth table to determine whether the following pair of compound sentences are logically equivalent: "p ≡ q" and "(q⊃p)&(p⊃q)."

ANALYSIS

After setting up a truth table for two letters, write A COLUMN FOR EACH SENTENCE:

		*			*
p	q	p≡q	q⊃p	p⊃q	(q⊃p)&(p⊃q)
t	t	t	t	t	t
f	t	f	f	t	f
t	f	f	t	f	f
f	f	t	t	t	t

Now CHECK THE ROWS on the two sentences. If they CORRESPOND in each case, the sentences are EQUIVALENT; if they DIFFER in any instance, the sentences are NOT EQUIVALENT. In this example, the two sentences are truth-functionally equivalent.

Use truth tables to determine whether the following sentences are equivalent.

1) "p&(qvr)" and "(p&q)v(p&r)" [371]   2) "-p&q" and "-(p&q)" [367]

E. TRUTH TABLE TEST FOR TAUTOLOGY AND CONTRADICTION

Our final application of truth tables involves TAUTOLOGY and CONTRADICTION.

A TAUTOLOGY is any sentence that is NECESSARILY TRUE because of its truth-functional form. A CONTRADICTION is any sentence that is NECESSARILY FALSE because of its truth-functional form.

We can use a truth table to determine whether a sentence is a tautology or a contradiction (or neither) by (1) setting up a column for the sentence in question, and (2) noting whether that column contains all t's, all f's, or a mixture of both. If the FINAL COLUMN is TRUE IN EVERY CASE, then the truth table has shown that the sentence is a TAUTOLOGY. If the final column is FALSE IN EVERY CASE, then the sentence is a CONTRADICTION. If the final column contains a mixture of both true and false cases, then the sentence is neither a tautology nor a contradiction.

EXAMPLE

Use a truth table to determine whether the following sentence is a tautology or a contradiction: $p \supset (pvq)$.

ANALYSIS

After setting up a column for the compound sentence, note whether the column contains all t's or all f's.

*

p	q	pvq	$p \supset (pvq)$
t	t	t	t
f	t	t	t
t	f	t	t
f	f	f	t

The final column is true in every case, so the truth table has shown that this sentence is necessarily true. Thus it is a tautology.

QUIZ 11

Use truth tables to determine whether the following sentences are tautologies or contradictions. 1. (pvq)&-(pvq) [370] 2. $p \supset p$ [368]

EXERCISE #4

Use truth tables to find the solutions to the following problems.

1. Is the following argument valid?
    If Swann is in love, Odette has returned his favors. Either Odette has not returned his favors or Swann is not in love. Therefore Swann is in love.
    Let S = "Swann is in love," let O = "Odette has returned his favors." (Hint: use "S" for the p column and "O" for the q column.) [379]
2. Is the negation of -(p&q) a contradiction? [383]
3. One way of demonstrating the validity of an argument is, first, to write the premises as a long conjunction that forms the antecedent of a conditional with the conclusion as the consequent. Then test the sentence to see if it is a tautology. If

the sentence is a tautology, then the argument is valid. If the sentence is not a tautology, then the argument is invalid.

Use this method to determine whether the following argument is valid or invalid.

p v q

-q

∴ p [387]

4. Are the following sentences logically equivalent? (A) "If Hemingway and Fitzgerald were of the lost generation, then Gertrude Stein was living in Paris." (B) "If Hemingway was of the lost generation then if Fitzgerald was of the lost generation, then Gertrude Stein was living in Paris."

(Let H = "Hemingway was of the lost generation," let F = "Fitzgerald was of the lost generation," and let G = "Gertrude Stein was living in Paris." Place "H" in the p column, "F" in the q column, and "G" in the r column.) [385]

5. Is it necessarily true that "If Ginsberg is a beat poet, then either Kerouac did not write *On the Road* or Ginsberg is a beat poet"? (Let G = "Ginsberg is a beat poet" and K = "Kerouac wrote *On the Road*." Place "G" in the p column and "K" in the q column.) [388]

6. Is the following argument valid?

If Clea marries Balthazar, then Justine is beautiful. Justine is beautiful. Therefore Clea marries Balthazar.

(Let C = "Clea marries Balthazar" and J = "Justine is beautiful." Place "C" in the p column and "J" in the q column.) [382]

7. Does the first sentence imply the second sentence? (A) "If Tolstoy wrote *Anna Karenina* then Mann wrote *The Magic Mountain*." (B) "If Mann wrote *The Magic Mountain* then Tolstoy wrote *Anna Karenina*. (Let T = "Tolstoy wrote *Anna Karenina*" and let M = "Mann wrote *The Magic Mountain*." Place "T" in the p column and "M" in the q column.) [386]

8. Are the following sentences logically equivalent? (A) "If Bloom eats the innards of fowls with relish, then Molly says 'Yes.'" (B) "Either it is not the case that Bloom eats the innards of fowls with relish or Molly says 'Yes.'" (Let B = "Bloom eats the innards of fowls with relish" and let M = "Molly says 'Yes.'" Place "B" in the p column and "M" in the q column.) [380]

9. Is the following argument valid or invalid?

Yossarian will escape from the army unless there is a Catch-22. Nurse Duckett declares Yossarian insane but there is a Catch-22. Therefore either there is a Catch-22 and Yossarian will not escape from the army or there is not a Catch-22 and Yossarian will escape from the army.

Let Y = "Yossarian will escape from the army," let C = "There is a Catch-22," and let D = "Nurse Duckett declares Yossarian insane." Place "Y" in the p column, "C" in the q column, and "D" in the r column.) [384]

10. Is this person saying something necessarily false? "If Jane Austen didn't write the *Tropic of Cancer* then Charles Bukowski wrote the Bible." (Let A = "Jane Austen wrote the *Tropic of Cancer*" and let B = "Charles Bukowski wrote the Bible." Place "A" in the p column and "B" in the q column.) [381]

Truth-Functional Principles for Use in Deduction

Elementary forms of valid argument

Modus
ponens: $p \supset q$, p; therefore q

Modus
tollens: $p \supset q$, $-q$; therefore $-p$

Chain
argument: $p \supset q$, $q \supset r$; therefore $p \supset r$

Disjunctive
arguments: $p \vee q$, $-p$; therefore q

$p \vee q$, $-q$ therefore p

p; therefore $p \vee q$ (*disjunctive addition*)

q; therefore $p \vee q$ (*disjunctive addition*)

Conjunctive
arguments: $-(p \,\&\, q)$, p; therefore $-q$

$-(p \,\&\, q)$, q; therefore $-p$

$p \,\&\, q$; therefore p (*simplification*)

$p \,\&\, q$; therefore q (*simplification*)

p, q; therefore $p \,\&\, q$ (*adjunction*)

Reductio ad
absurdum: $p \supset -p$; therefore $-p$

$p \supset (q \,\&\, -q)$; therefore $-p$

Dilemmas: $p \supset q$, $r \supset q$, $p \vee r$; therefore q
(*simple constructive*)

$p \supset q$, $p \supset r$, $-q \vee -r$; therefore $-p$
(*simple destructive*)

$p \supset q$, $r \supset s$, $p \vee r$; therefore $q \vee s$
(*complex constructive*)

$p \supset q$, $r \supset s$, $-q \vee -s$; therefore $-p \vee -r$
(*complex destructive*)